Bríd Keeley is a psychic healer from the ... channelling healing she experiences her clients' physical and emotional pain. Bríd has the ability to communicate with the dead and frequently assists trapped souls on their journey home.

Bríd (pronounced *Breed*) takes no credit for her perceptive ability and clarity while channelling healings. During this process she is able to see into the depths of the soul. She sees where we lock the things away that still trouble us and, subconsciously but ultimately, influence our lives. She gently guides us through the process of releasing these burdens.

In this book she brings her message and knowledge to a wider audience. Her hope is to help the reader's soul on the ups and downs of their journey through life.

Bríd tells us "our ship is in". It is up to us whether we take the journey or remain waiting on the shore.

MEMORIES AND MISSIONS

BRÍD KEELEY

MEMORIES AND MISSIONS

Vanguard Press

VANGUARD PAPERBACK

ISBN 978 178465 064 3

*Vanguard Press is an imprint of
Pegasus Elliot MacKenzie Publishers Ltd.*
www.pegasuspublishers.com

First Published in 2015

**Vanguard Press
Sheraton House Castle Park
Cambridge England**

Printed & Bound in Great Britain

This book is in memory of my late grand-aunt, Biddy, a wonderful woman and healer in her own right.

Acknowledgements

I sincerely thank all those who took the time to write their very personal stories and testimonials which form such an integral part of this book.

Thanks Bernie, for all your hard work editing and correcting my many literary errors; Mary and Dermot, for helping put my thoughts in order and my publishers for making my dream a reality.

I would also like to acknowledge my dear friends: Mai and John, for your encouragement, and Sarah, for all the laughter along the way.

CONTENTS

FOREWORD

Welcome to my world. I was born in 1967 on a small dairy farm in the west of Ireland, a middle child (or as middle as you can be as one of eight children). To the outside observer my life may seem to be unremarkable, but this is not the case. I am a spiritual healer.

I channel healing by praying for divine intervention. The healing requested can be for one's mind, body or soul.

For as long as I have been channelling healing, my clients have repeatedly asked me similar types of questions:

"How does the healing work?"

"Who does the healing?"

"Have you always had this gift?"

"How did it affect you as a child?"

"Do you see dead people?"

"What happens when we die?"

In this book I endeavour to answer these questions. If you are open to the possibility that: there is a higher power; when we die there is a 'something else'; we all have angels; guides and spirits waiting to help us. Then I may have the answers to these questions.

Clients generally come to see me in relation to physical health conditions but when we start the healing process what we inevitably find ourselves working on is a greater need for emotional or spiritual healing. I have found that clients frequently come with similar types of issues around life lessons, perceptions and heartache, presenting with different aspects of the same problems.

I have come to understand that the bonds we form while alive transcend death. Those that loved us, who have since died, still love us even after their time here ends. They would like us to be the best we can be and to know that we still have the same connection with them. As we heal and overcome our inherited issues this in turn helps our ancestors, as it eases their regrets for conditioning us to their limiting beliefs. Our progression in turn helps their progression.

My work as a spiritual healer also involves assisting trapped spirits (or ghosts, as they are more commonly known). These trapped spirits also need help releasing the issues and the cords that bind them to this world. In this book I explain how I work with these spirits: to identify what is stopping their progression; how, with the help of Archangel Michael, I cut those cords and facilitate a crossing (the releasing of a trapped earthbound spirit).

Often we don't see things as they are; we see things as we perceive them to be. Therefore, rather than fill this book with recollections of healings and crossings as experienced through my perception, I have asked clients, friends and students to tell their stories of the events they witnessed *(these are inserted throughout the book; they are in italics to differentiate them from my own entries).*

As some of the stories and examples are of a very personal nature I have, on occasion, changed names and some individual details to protect identity.

I hope you enjoy my endeavours to explain the importance of spiritual healing for both the living and the dead and that it proves thought provoking for you and maybe you will find some personal healing along the way.

When I refer to 'God' at any stage throughout this book I am referring to the God of my understanding. My own understanding of God is limited to the knowledge that has been passed on to me and from my own life experiences. It is for each of us to come to our own understanding.

"Believe nothing, no matter where you read it, or who said it, no matter if I have said it, unless it agrees with your own reason and your own common sense." – Buddha.

A SENSITIVE CHILD

As a child the main difference between me and the majority of other children was that I was very sensitive. I mean very sensitive; I felt everything. It is really only in the last fifteen years that I have come to fully understand this sensitivity. I am clairsentient.

Some people are clairvoyant. This is probably the gift most of us are familiar with. True clairvoyants can see past and future events "You are going to meet a tall, dark, handsome man and live happily ever after." "You are going to get promoted at work" etc. Other people are clairaudient, meaning they hear messages. Again this can be past information and sometimes present or future information. If they use this gift to work as a medium, they may channel verbal messages from those passed on, or from their angels or guides.

My strongest psychic gift is my clairsentient ability. It means I feel things. I describe it to my clients as being like a human x-ray machine. If someone I am with is sad, I feel sad. If they have a pain in their back, I feel that pain in my back. If they have toothache, I feel the toothache and so on.

I now know that I can switch on and switch off this process. Now I only use this gift while channelling healing for clients. Otherwise it can be exhausting and, more importantly, it feels like I am intruding on people's personal lives without their knowledge or permission. I feel if I tune into someone else's energy without being asked it would be like looking through someone's handbag while they have gone to the bathroom. I have no right to know anyone else's issues or how they are really feeling unless they give me permission to 'tune in'.

As a child, however, I was not equipped with the knowledge I now have. I did not know that the pain I felt was someone else's pain/sorrow and could not work out why I was so sad. I did not know that it was possible to switch on and switch off. I would have woken up happy; I was never keen on going to school but would have been feeling OK until I got on the school bus or into the classroom when I could suddenly feel close to tears for no apparent reason.

This gift got me in trouble at school on more than one occasion. Unfortunately, many of the nuns in the primary school I attended believed in the principle that if you spare the rod you spoil the child. That said there was one lovely lay teacher and a really kind nun who taught me for some of my time in primary; my only happy memories from that school were during those years.

On a number of occasions when other children in my class room were being disciplined/beaten and humiliated I would feel both their physical pain and their emotional pain at the injustice of the situation along with my own feelings at witnessing these events. More than once I went to the aid of other children only to be punished for interfering and so would have my own pain as well as theirs to contend with.

Occasionally, children from the Travelling Community would attend our school. The Travelling Community at that time were true travellers in every sense of the word and would never stay at any location for more than a few weeks. Their children would attend school for short periods of time depending on where the family had set up temporary camp. As these children were so far behind in their education they would be placed in classes where the other children were years younger than them. One of the nuns had told us we were not to mix with them as they would be a bad influence on us.

I remember three girls from the Travelling Community arriving at our school when I was about six or seven. I felt so bad for them; they looked between three and six years older than the children in our classroom. Because they were so behind for their age, having missed so much school, they were frequently unable to answer teacher's questions. Therefore, they were getting constant beatings from our nun. I felt sad, angry, confused, proud, but at the time didn't know it was their feelings I was getting.

Even at that young age I was very aware of the injustice in the way these children were treated in school. So, at break time, I went over to play with them. I still remember their faces when I went over. They didn't speak and I didn't speak; I just took turns with them swinging on a pole. But it was like we were communicating without words. In my mind I was saying "This is wrong the way you are being treated and I will stand with you". I felt they were saying, "You are not supposed to be here; don't you all hate us? You will get in trouble; thank you". I could feel my classmates emotions too: shock, fear and confusion. I also felt the pain when the nun hit me for playing with the travelling children.

It was about that time, at the age of six, I decided that I would never cry again. I really believed that the beatings, I and some of the other children were getting, were wrong. Especially as there were some children who were never hit. It seemed to me that it depended on your address and who your parents were. Punishments took different forms, from emotional punishment: being mocked and humiliated by the teacher, to physical punishment: having your ear pulled, smacked, or hit with a stick.

In first class we would get spelling and maths tests and would get one slap for every wrong answer. Because this resulted in so many slaps the nun would use a stick to save her hands. I worked hard and was good at my maths but terrible at spelling. (In my twenties I discovered, to my relief, that I am dyslexic, as up until then I had believed what some of the nuns had told me, that I was thick and stupid.) So, as a six-year-old it didn't make any difference how long I spent at homework trying to learn the spellings, as the next day I would reverse the letters. Often with results of up to five incorrect spellings out of the ten words we had been given to learn, with one slap for each of the five errors.

I knew something was wrong with the system and that I was not a bad child. I also knew that these daily beatings were not improving my ability to spell. I was a defenceless, quiet child and the only way I could stand up for myself was not to cry. This infuriated the nun and she would hit me even harder, but I would just stand there and stare at her. I could feel the anger and frustration welling up in her. I was never destined to be the teacher's pet!

Unfortunately, ours was not the only school in Ireland to have these types of experiences. For many children from previous generations the punishments were much more severe. The fear, injustice and oppression can still be felt in those buildings. Sensitive children now attending school in these old buildings, although no longer subjected to abuse, can still feel the emotions from just being there. This is similar to when you enter a room and know that there has just been an argument. Although you have not witnessed this, you are aware of the energy in the room as you can feel it. These negative emotions can also attach to any physical object, belongings, furniture, jewellery and clothing etc. It would be a huge help for these sensitive children to learn to ground and protect themselves.

When they are older they may learn how to clear an area or building of all its old negative energy. Even opening a window and stating your intention of letting go any blocked energy is a big help to improving the energy in a room.

I try to open the windows in my home as much as possible and have got into the habit of saying little mantras when I do so. It can be something like:

***

I release the tears and fears and replace them with love, joy and laughter.

I release all poverty thinking and replace it with prosperity thinking (I tend to say this behind my front door where the bills are usually waiting for me!)

I release all thoughts and feelings of illness and disease and replace them with good health.

I release any feelings of anger and resentment and replace them with forgiveness and love.

I release all feelings of disappointment and replace them with trust in life to bring my Highest Spiritual Good to me at all times.

I release all feelings of fear and replace them with strength and courage.

I release all feelings of lack and replace them with God's abundant grace.

I know I am blessed beyond my fondest dreams.

I release all blocks and replace them with God's love.

*****

The mantra can be anything you like, the objective being to release any negative energy and replace it with good. Think about what is going on in your home/work space and decide what negative energies need to be released and then remember to put something back in its place, usually the opposite of what you want gone. The following testimonial submitted by a client goes some way towards explaining the type of things that can happen when I am asked to do a house clearance.

THE HOME PLACE

Anne

Following the passing of both my parents within a twelve month period, I was undoubtedly at one of the lowest points of my life. I was immersed in the depths of sadness and grief. I was, and am to this day, fortunate to have wonderful, supportive friends who journeyed with me through the dark days. Among them was my dear friend, Bríd, who conducted many healing sessions, which I found to be comforting and uplifting.

The knowledge and reassurance that Mam and Dad are still guiding me, in my present life, was amazing and almost unbelievable at the start. For instance, Bríd saw in her mind's eye a pile of earth and a shovel outside my parents' house. Bríd had never been to their home but was able to describe it to me. Also she could not have known that my dad would always choose the shovel as his tool, even if a digger was needed!

I had been considering since their passing to refurbish their house. The description of the shovel to me seemed to signify my dad's desire for me to commence the refurbishing of the family home! With the help of family and good friends the dream/vision became a reality. At the time, I had no idea of just how much healing the project itself would bring me.

Following my parents' death, the home place had been rented for a short period. Following the departure of the tenant, who was suffering from depression, Bríd felt that a clearing of the house would be beneficial before the refurbishment commenced. She willingly came one Sunday. When she arrived, she informed me that there was a trapped spirit visiting the house, a former occupant of a nearby derelict house. Bríd calmly prepared to do the crossing prayers. Remarkably, the music, which I had been playing on a cassette player, started acting up very strangely. It started playing really quickly and then really slowly; then quickly again. It was a little weird for my liking but Bríd reassured me that everything was OK and that the spirit was just trying to get our attention so that we would help her.

Bríd had a vision of an elderly, stooped woman. Then she could see the same woman in her youth as a beautiful tall young woman dancing at a party in my parents' house. There was much fun and gaiety. Then, as the dancing stopped, a man dressed in a suit, a hat and wellington boots came cycling to the front door to meet this woman and to lovingly help her cross home to the light. Bríd then explained in detail everything she had seen.

The woman was unfamiliar to me but I recognised the man immediately as Martin from next door, long since dead. He was an old man when I was a child and I often visited him as he lived alone. It was one of my childhood memories that he would wear the suit when going out anywhere but then would put his wellington boots on over it.

I was curious as to who the woman was, but shortly afterwards my Aunt in America threw some light on it. Apparently the woman's name was Mary. Her husband Pat was Martin's uncle. The couple had no children but were very well liked and wereu good neighbours. They had invited

Martin to live with them and had signed their place over to him. Not long after Pat died, there was a wedding in our house with music, song and dance.

Mary did not attend as she was in mourning and in fact was upset and offended that the house wedding party was taking place at all. She said at the time that it felt like they were dancing on his grave. This sadly caused a rift between the two households and the longstanding friendship was strained.

Mary was never again to dance as she had so often done in our house. It is likely that Mary regretted her harsh words but, through her stubbornness, was unable to rectify the situation. At the time of her death, some years later, she had chosen not to cross on. She had still felt disrespected but also regretted the anger and resentment she had held towards my parents. She had been unable to cut these emotional cords following her death.

Coincidently, she died on the exact day and month of my son's birthday and she and Pat were godparents to my dad. Some time later, on going through old photographs of my mother's, I found a photo of Mary which I have included in my family's scrapbook of old photos. I now make a point of lighting a candle for her on my son's birthday and wishing her well.

Bríd then set about the job she had called to do that day, which was to clear the house of all blocked energy. She explained that it was just the negative energy she was clearing and that was what she was going to pick up on. She would not be clearing the positive love and laughter the house had known. She explained that buildings hold memories and that it is nothing to be frightened of. It was similar to my dad leaving his clothes behind. So, instead of removing old clothes, we would be removing blocked energy.

Bríd had never been there before but as she went from room to room she described firstly the symptoms my dad had with his emphysema in the bedroom where he had lived out his final years in. She described my mother's symptoms. She also picked up on the tenant's sadness and depression which was mainly in the bedroom but also in the bathroom. Bríd explained that, as we wash in the bath or shower, often we can leave negative memories there. We agreed on the mantra Bríd would use: "I release all blockages and memories of ill health replacing them with joy, love and laughter".

On finishing, Bríd suggested I dispose of a towel that was in the bathroom. There were other towels and bed linen in the house from my parents' time and all the items in the kitchen were also belonging to my parents. Again Bríd had no way of knowing that this was the only item left in the property by the tenant. This really shocked me but again proved that she was being directed in her work.

Bríd then described happy memories from the house, memories I had long forgotten. One was of me standing on a stool to be able to stand beside my grandfather and to look at his pocket watch. Another was of my mam standing at the kitchen window watching my sister and me playing outside. She even described the dresses we were wearing and, yes she was right, we did have those clothes.

Bríd then passed on suggestions from my dad about the drainage that he felt was needed for the refurbishment. She *asked if I was aware of a spring on the property as my dad was showing suggestions for a drainage system that would lead to and empty into the spring. He also gave a suggestion about where the new stairs should go. He felt that an old tree would have to be cut to make way for the development and, if possible, he would like the wood used in the refurbishment.*

I am delighted that I have been able to do this. I have used it in window sills, and had a new dresser made for the kitchen. I love the refurbishment all the more, knowing that I have Mam and Dad's approval. It was an amazing experience, firstly helping Mary to cross to the light. Also, witnessing the house clearing and the evidence from my parents and grandfather of their continuing presence in my life.

The next day my engineer called with a drawing showing his suggested drainage system. An exact copy of what Bríd had explained the day before feeding into the spring. The engineer had also been having difficulty trying to fit the stairs to connect the old part of the house with the extension that I wanted. I told him about Dad's suggestion and he was flabbergasted. He went and took measurements and yes we now have the stairs, as per dad's idea.

A DIFFERENT CHILDHOOD

It was like a game, sitting at the breakfast table recounting dreams from the previous night. They were usually insignificant dreams, like distant relatives that we had not seen for a while, who would then surprise our family with an unplanned visit the day after my dream. Other family members may have also dreamt and so it was sometimes like a competition. The game continued into my teenage years.

Then, in my mid-teens, a dream I had made me realise this was a game I no longer wanted to play. In my dream a family member had died yet no one within the family was crying. I didn't recount my dream at breakfast the next morning but secretly was in dread of what the day held. When my father returned from the creamery, he told us an elderly relative of his had died. This probably sounds terrible but I was so relieved. I had only met this particular relative on a few occasions and even my father did not have a lot of contact with her. Even though I was relieved, I was also scared by the events of the day. That night I prayed more earnestly than I had ever done before. I prayed that this gift be taken away and that I would no longer have such vivid dreams, for now at least, or until such time as I was more equipped to deal with their implications. My prayers were answered and my dreams did not return until five years later.

I have very few memories of my time in secondary school. Somehow I went from an emotional sponge in primary to becoming a shy student that blocked everything out, good and bad. It was a real shock to me on my final day in school when fellow students were hugging me and saying how much they would miss me, as I was feeling nothing. I had not even considered that I should be feeling emotional that day, which to everyone else seemed to be a big event.

It was much later in my adult life that I have learnt that in order to live I have to feel; otherwise, I was missing the point to living. I thought there must be something wrong with me, as emotions seemed to come so easy to everyone else. Subconsciously I had decided that in order to block out the pain and emotions of others in my immediate surroundings I had to emotionally shut down. I look back with a sense of loss for those years. I also think it put me at a disadvantage in preparation for the adult world that I was to be faced with when I later moved to live in London.

I believe we are here to experience life, to feel the joy and the pain, the good and the bad in order to learn and grow. We need to embrace life and make the most of it while staying positive. When we succeed and take what may seem like insignificant steps we are improving our own lives. We will also be better able to help future generations by not passing on so many limiting beliefs. At the same time, we are easing the regrets of the generations gone before us, who in turn passed these beliefs on to us. I truly believe that as the living heal, and make progress by releasing their inherited beliefs, this in turn brings healing and lessens the guilt of those generations that have gone before us.

By the time I started socialising at the age of seventeen I was learning to open up to experiencing feelings and learning to express my emotions. I still had not worked out how to do this without feeling the emotions of those in my proximity. The social scene proved a huge challenge to me. This is possibly true for everyone: as we start to socialise we have to learn how to fit in to this new environment. At discos I felt most comfortable staying as near as possible to the exit doors or any area that wasn't very crowded so that I had less energy to pick up on.

My biggest problem is that I love music and I love to dance. This caused a predicament that, to this day, I still haven't quite worked out how to overcome. When dancing, I let all my protective layers down so that I am open to feel the music and the freedom of expression in dancing. In doing so I would be swamped with so many feelings: excitement, happiness and joy. But also, as others drank alcohol and let down their inhibitions, their negative feelings: frustrations, dislikes, sadness, fears etc., were all exposed to me.

I remember a teenage boy from the area I grew up in; he was extremely handsome and would frequently have girls competing for his attention. He was always smiling and charismatic yet I never wanted to be in his company as I would feel both anger and, at the same time, tears of sadness. As soon as he entered a venue I knew he was there, even if I didn't see or meet him. It was many years later as I got to know him better and understand myself better that I discovered he was from a very difficult abusive home situation but he had learnt at an early age to mask his feelings to others.

Whenever I became overwhelmed by the various emotions I was picking up in the nightclubs I would return to the safety of a quieter part of the venue. This didn't really help my love life as there was no way I could explain this to anyone else. Often boys (that I would have thought really cute) would ask me to dance but I would have to make up some sort of excuse. They generally were not impressed with my poor excuses and would find someone else to take dancing and then asked the other girls out on dates.

TIME TO GROW UP

I completed a two year secretarial course in 1987 in the midst of a national depression. There were sixty students in my year; the majority of us emigrated. Some to America, Australia or France, but most of us went to England.

I had some fast growing up to do, coming from a farm in rural Ireland and then landing a job with a stock-broking firm. I had never been the girlie girl. I owned one suit, which I had worn to my interview and now needed to fit into the world of makeup, suits and briefcases. I had never been in a lift, never eaten at a restaurant; I had never heard of fast food or frozen meals. My parents had only got a house phone connected at our home about a year prior to my leaving; now I was surrounded by computer screens, phones and telex machines. There was a real buzz and lots of activity. I had got a job as a secretary but during my first week had managed to get transferred over to being responsible for trade settlements. I did not have to worry about my spellings; instead, my days were full of maths calculations and watching share trades on the computer screens.

My new life could not have been further removed from my childhood but I came to love it. Approximately two years after arriving in London, the dreams started again.

They started off with little insignificant things but got very serious very quickly. London was in the midst of IRA bombings and hoax calls. In one vivid dream, I was on an underground train going to work when the alarm sounded. Everyone started to leave the trains and exit the underground. I could see a child crying but I couldn't get to him. Then I was outside looking at snakes!

The next morning I followed my normal routine and had got about half way to work when the alarm sounded. The train stopped and everyone had to leave the station immediately. Being true "Brits", no one ran and people left in an orderly fashion. But I could feel their panic and I talked myself into calming down. Two days earlier, a bomb alert had turned out not to have been a hoax and had resulted in real casualties.

In my carriage that morning there had been an unaccompanied boy of about twelve on his way to school. When the alarm sounded he had started to cry. The passage way was very busy with everyone rushing past and he just stood flat against the wall, crying. I couldn't get to him as I would have to go against the crowd. As I was looking back, a female underground station guard found him and took his hand and led him out.

I knew the panic I felt was not mine and told myself to release it as in my dream I had been standing outside. I was a bit worried about the snakes though! Thankfully, the bomb scare that morning was a hoax and when I got outside there was a statue with a metal railing around it. There was a snake carved on the top of each rail!

A few weeks later and another dream about the bombings; this time I heard an explosion, I could see metal bent back and blood on it. Then I saw hundreds and hundreds of rats running up from the tunnels. When I woke the next morning, I was really put out by the dream and ended up being a few minutes later than normal. As the tube I was on neared my destination of Victoria Station we came to a sudden stop. The tube stayed in the tunnel for about twenty minutes. Then it reversed to the previous station of Green Park.

There was very little information available as to why we were returned to Green Park, other than Victoria Station was now closed. I got out at the park and enjoyed my unexpected stroll across the park and then on to Victoria. On arrival I discovered a bomb had gone off in the station. It had been placed in a metal rubbish bin and resulted in serious injuries. Following the explosion, hundreds of rats had run up from the tunnel. My dream had again played out.

I was really upset and confused. What was the point of seeing the explosion in my dream if I had not been shown enough information about when and where exactly the bomb had been hidden? Also, with my Irish accent, I really was not going to be able to go to a police station and say, "I had a dream about a bomb," as chances were I would have been locked up. That night I prayed again for these dreams to stop, and that if I was to have a special gift could it be one I could use.

One evening on my way home from work I stopped at the bank-link machine to check my balance. These machines at the time had a plastic cover that came up half way when you started the transaction. As I entered my pin number I saw a reflection of a man standing directly behind me moving his hands towards my throat. Somehow I managed to get my hands up, inside his, before he could tighten his grip. He seemed so strong but somehow I was able to push his hands out and away from my neck. He stared at me with a really stunned look and ran away. At the time, I thought that the early warning, seeing his reflection on the plastic screen, saved my life. But, thinking back, there is no way I was stronger than him. I still question if I received divine assistance that day.

The events of that night really affected my confidence. If I just had to walk past a bank machine it would be enough to start me crying. I decided to take some time out of London, with its crowded streets and busy subways, to reconnect with nature and the land. My boyfriend and I signed on with an agency and were placed with a family in the Negev desert in Israel, working in their greenhouses.

On our days off we got to explore the towns and countryside. Prior to this, I had almost considered the biblical stories as fairy tales. Now I found myself considering what the significance of these stories was for me. I was able to walk the last walk Jesus took in his life. To see and touch the walls of the house where Mary grew up. I had the opportunity to sit under the olive trees in the Garden of Gethsemane. I got to visit the towns of Bethlehem, Nazareth and Galilee. All of these experiences opened a deep connection to God for me and what I believe in. My daily prayers now took on a deeper and more significant meaning. They were no longer words chanted like childhood rhymes. Instead, I now felt a connection with each word.

After six months in Israel I was ready to return to the action and excitement of London. On our return, my boyfriend and I agreed to go our separate ways. In 1995 I got married and in 1997 my husband and I moved from London to a beautiful town in Essex. We bought a property on the suburb of the town and I could once again spend time daily in nature. There were lovely walks just minutes from the house where our dog and I would spend many happy hours in the nearby woods and along the river banks. This time in nature also gave me the opportunity to pray and meditate which I believe was part of the key to the way my gift was about to develop and how my life would change forever as a result of this new dimension of my gift.

When living in London, one of my closest friends was an Irish girl, Teresa. We clicked as soon as we met and enjoyed many outings and chats over tea. However, when I moved to Israel, I lost contact with her and later discovered she had emigrated to America. Unexpectedly, I got to meet up with her during the summer of 2012 and as we chatted we discovered we both had a huge interest in spirituality. We were both surprised that we had not been able to share this with each other in our early twenties. I found it reassuring that, without even realising it, our relationship was based on a much deeper connection and that we will always be drawn to like-minded people even if we don't realise it at the time.

REUNIONS

Meeting up with Bríd after more than a twenty year separation was an amazing experience, first to learn that she is a practising spiritual healer and quite intuitive to boot. In my very short visit she gave me a healing session. This included physical healing where I could feel heat over various parts of my body. She was able to tell me I had two people looking out for me in the spirit world. At the time I could not associate the names she gave me. Later I confirmed these names to be my long forgotten grandfather and grand-uncle. It was great to learn that these men I had briefly known in my early childhood cared about me and were looking out for me. Our connections live on long after we are deceased. It was a wonderful experience and I can't wait to go back for more.

CASPER

In the autumn of '97 my kid sister Bernie (ten years my junior) had taken a year out from college. She was now working in London as a live-in bar girl. The first opportunity I got, I arranged to come and visit her. We spent a lovely day exploring the nearby market and pottering around the local shops. That night I stayed over with her in her room. It was a really long, large, bright room and had a spare bed.

I was soon asleep, but not for long. I could hear a man breathing. I sat bolt upright in bed. He (or it) was standing at the foot of Bernie's bed. I am not sure how to describe him. He looked human but there was a dark shadow around him that came out about two inches from his entire body. His clothes were definitely not from this century: he wore a white frilly shirt, with long, loose sleeves and his trousers were more like riding jodhpers. He did not move, look around or acknowledge me. He just stood looking down at my sister, as if protecting her. Needless to say, I didn't sleep or try to. I just sat upright for the night, transfixed by what I was seeing in front of me and trying to decide what to say to my sister.

At daylight he disappeared. After breakfast I got the train home, having said nothing to my sister, not wanting to frighten her. I certainly wouldn't want to live somewhere haunted. I had never been one for watching horror movies but, what little bits I had seen, the ghost generally was the baddie in the movie. But this didn't feel like that and I really believed this spirit meant my sister no harm.

Two weeks later Bernie invited me to visit her again. I declined staying overnight and arranged to meet her at the train station rather than meeting her at her place. I know I am her big sister and therefore supposed to look out and protect her but there is a limit! Bernie seemed preoccupied at first and we chatted about the usual trivial day-to-day bits and pieces. Then she said, "This is going to sound weird but I think the pub and lodgings are haunted. I keep thinking there is someone behind me: I hear footsteps but there is no one there."

Not being able to keep my secret any longer I blurted out the events of my previous visit. Forgetting that my story really was not the reassurance she needed from her big sister that everything would be OK. Once I stopped talking long enough to see the look of anxiety and fear on her face I found myself promising that I would get help and answers. Where I was going to get those answers from, at that stage, I had no idea.

On my way home I remembered that one of my neighbours was friends with a psychic. I called around to my neighbours the next day and got the telephone number. I phoned the psychic and asked to make an appointment for my sister. She said she was fully booked for the next two months. All sorts of conversations were going on in my brain. "What do I do now?" I had promised my sister help and failing this I had no idea what to do.

The psychic then cut across my thoughts unprompted: "Tell your sister he means her no harm. He killed himself because of unrequited love; your sister reminds him of the woman he loved. He means her no harm."

I thanked her and said goodbye. At this point I didn't know which was freaking me out more – the ghost or the psychic. I phoned Bernie; she was a little reassured but not much. I didn't visit her again for a couple of months.

In the meantime Bernie and Casper (as we came to call him) had come to an understanding. Bernie had put down a few miserable days and nights with toothache. She had been lying in bed exhausted from lack of sleep and pain. Casper had come to visit her in the bedroom. Although she couldn't see him, at that stage, he was making his presence known by walking loudly back and forth on her wooden bedroom floor. Bernie, finally at breaking point, sat up and shouted at him. She explained quite forcefully that she had no problem sharing with him but he had to respect her privacy and right now she was in pain so back off. He did.

As their unusual friendship grew, his cheeky sense of humour came to the fore. She would be busy serving in the pub when she'd see someone's arm waving constantly for attention. Thinking it was someone waiting to be served in the busy bar she would go to that spot to discover 'no one'. Casper, now aware that Bernie could see him, was enjoying his new friendship. He started playing tricks on other staff members. Other live-in bar girls would wake to their feet being tickled; footsteps would be heard upstairs during the day when there was no one in the living accommodation.

One night the manager had agreed to a lock-in for half a dozen locals. One local man, on his way to the bathroom, acknowledged the barman waving at him. He got quite a shock when he realised that it was not the bar man but a ghost that was waving at him. His friends teased him that the only spirits he had seen that night were in a whisky glass.

Then it came time for Bernie to leave and return to college. She told Casper she was moving on and hoped he would also be able to move on and find peace. From time to time Bernie would check in by phone to some of the staff who would update her on Casper's latest antics and jokes. Sadly he had not moved on.

Now when I see trapped spirits I see them exactly as they would have looked during their life here on earth. I no longer see a shadow around their outline. Sometimes I am taken by surprise when I realise the person who is now standing beside me, and in many cases speaking directly to me, is in fact someone who is deceased.

Thankfully, most trapped spirits I have encountered since meeting Casper are ready to move on. This is generally why they have come to my attention, because they want me to facilitate their crossing. But, unfortunately, there have been some instances like Casper where they have chosen to remain held in this world instead of crossing to the light, preventing their souls from making any further progress.

I have read various autobiographies of people who are psychic. All with amazing gifts, but the part of their stories that surprises me most is that many of them had been seeing spirits, angels and/or ghosts since they were children. My encounter with Casper was the first time I had seen anything supernatural.

I was in my early thirties and I was absolutely terrified on that first encounter. I have no idea how all these people, whose gifts were so strong from early childhood, had been equipped to deal with it as children. Now in my forties I can say that I am very comfortable communicating with the spirit world while working with clients during spiritual healing.

Some people have said to me that ghosts are evil and I should have nothing to do with them; that I should be protecting myself from these lower energy levels. I do accept that some can be evil but thankfully it is very unusual to encounter evil. My reply to these people is "How many pure evil people do you know?" Their answer has always been "none".

When people die they do not change their personality. If, for example, while alive someone is a fun loving teenager, whose worst offence was skipping school, having the music up too loud in their bedrooms, and not always judging how much alcohol their bodies could take. If this teenager, for whatever reason, decides to commit suicide and chooses not to go to the light at the time of their death, they do not suddenly change personality and become like the poltergeists we see in Halloween horror movies.

There are still occasions when I come into the presence of trapped souls that I would sooner pretend that I am imagining it. For example, when I wake up in the middle of the night to hear footsteps in my hallway. While still half asleep, my mind tries to work out whether someone has broken into my home, then I realise, no it's just a dead person looking for help. On accepting the second option I have on occasion put my head under the blankets hoping whoever it is will just disappear. I then feel guilty; I end up apologising and agree to help. I take a moment to ask for protection for myself and protection for the soul.

There are many ways to ground and protect ourselves. For me, it is the belief in the process that matters. If you believe that by blessing yourself with holy water, or carrying a blessed medal, wearing silver, picturing yourself in a bubble or tent, saying prayers, mantras, affirmations or whatever method you choose is going to protect you, it will. As long as you truly believe this, you will be protected.

Once I feel safe I then have a conversation with the trapped spirit. This may be in spoken words; or the conversation can be communicated through our thoughts, or in picture format in my mind. I learn their individual circumstances and why they have not crossed to the light. It only takes a few minutes of my time to stop and listen to their unique story. I then explain to them how much God loves them and he does not want them to suffer like this. I encourage them to go to the light. I always feel honoured and humbled that they have chosen me to help them.

During the time when a spirit is crossing over there is the most overwhelming feeling of love from those that have come forward to bring their loved ones home to the light. I feel privileged to be part of the process and to feel that love. On the rare occasion that they decline to cross to the light I certainly will not exorcise them from the area, no more than I would make a living teenager homeless. I am very comfortable with this belief system now but back when I first encountered Casper I was struggling to make sense of it all.

A NEW GIFT

In the winter of '99, at the age of thirty-two, I took night classes in massage. I thought this would be a nice way to relax after my hectic days in the office. The course was for personal use and not certified and therefore we had no study or exams to do. During the course I started to notice other class members' pains. If we were working on shoulders I might get a temporary pain in my neck or knee. By now I understood that these were not my pains but those of whomever I was working on. I would discreetly put my hand over the area I knew was in pain or diseased and feel a heat leave my hand. I got some strange looks from the people I was doing treatments for. Thankfully no one asked me questions as I would not have been able to answer them.

Having finished the course I went on to do a diploma in massage and aromatherapy and again loved it. I knew that when I was giving a massage healing was coming through me, but still did not fully understand how or why this was happening. On one occasion when I gave a back massage the lady commented that it was the most amazing massage she had ever had. She said that at times, if she did not know better, she would have thought there were two people giving the massage at the same time!

I had decided only to practise on friends and family as I did not fully understand what was happening and carried on like this for a few years. At this stage it was becoming commonplace for spirits to appear while I was giving treatments and because it was only friends and family I was practising on I felt free to pass on their messages.

The next course I took was in Reiki. My plan was that I would then tell people I was doing Reiki and this would kind of explain the extra experiences that were happening.

In 2000, I returned to Ireland to live in a rural village in The Midlands. After so many years of city life I immediately fell in love with the beautiful countryside, surrounded by the mountains and forestry and fresh air. I became a regular walker and again I was able to connect back to nature. I didn't know anyone in the area but over time I began to settle into the community. I had again let my gift shut down as, living in a new place, I didn't feel I could share this part of me with strangers.

I got chatting one day to a local woman that I had met once at a social occasion. She had been having a tough time of late and her life had become very difficult. I found myself offering to do healing for her and she took me up on the offer. The healing session went really well and I passed on what information I was given and we could both feel the healing energy coming through. Later that day I was filled with doubts about what I was doing. Was I playing God? Did I have any right to ask God and the angels to help people. Should I be intervening in other people's life journeys? I got myself into a total tizzy.

The next day the woman came back. She said she felt so much stronger and at peace in herself. She thanked me for my help and asked me to book in four other friends and family members for healing sessions.

I think that was the single most important moment in my journey to becoming a spiritual healing practitioner. Helping me open up to channelling healing for others and to finally accepting my gift. I no longer kept it a secret. I was prepared to share it with those who needed it most.

From then on my reputation has spread by word of mouth and personal recommendations. When clients come to me for the first time I try to explain to them what it is I do and how it works; I still struggle to put it into words. No two clients will have the same experience. Even the same client on a repeat visit will have a different experience. The only thing they all have in common is they are left with a feeling of peace.

Sometimes the healing will totally concentrate on physical healing. Other times it will be evidence from the spirit world. Sometimes it will be emotional healing where the client feels safe to open an old wound or secret and let the pain out of their hearts. It is never the same and again I feel privileged to play my small part in the process. I am always reminding people that it is not me that is responsible for any healing received. It is as if I put in the phone call for the client, similar to a switchboard operator, except I am calling God.

I begin each session by praying that the client will receive healing, love and evidence. I finish the session with gratitude for the healing received and ask God to keep the client in His love and care.

Originally I was very specific in my healing requests, "Please help ease the pain in Mary's back." "Please increase Joe's energy levels." "Please help Kate let go of her anger." Over time I have learnt to leave it to the powers that be. Now I simply ask for whatever healing is in the person's best interest. By being too specific I might be blocking healing to the area that in fact needs it most. Mary's back pain may be coming from her hip, while John's energy may be low because he is not sleeping, and so on.

Channelling healing is like saying a prayer or affirmation. We need to believe our requests will be heard. For example I don't like storms. I used to lie awake all night during storms, frantically praying that 'me and mine' would be protected. Now if there is a storm I give thanks that all is well, safe, blessed and protected and I sleep much better. We have to trust in the process and release it.

This healing journey has brought me to the understanding that we are all connected. Frequently I see that, as the client heals, it inevitably has a positive effect on their deceased loved ones in spirit. Generally our parents and guardians did the best they could for us with their life experiences and their understanding of the world and this has gone a long way towards shaping us to be the individuals we are today. When our parents pass on to the spirit world they may become aware of how some of their actions or beliefs have had a negative impact on our lives. As we heal and release these beliefs this in turn allows not just our progress but also progress for those who instilled these limiting belief systems on us.

For example it may be the over protective mother who does not want her children mixing with children that are not from similar backgrounds. This can, in later life, hinder the young adult when entering the world of work and/or in their social lives. The mother believed, with her limited life experiences, that she was protecting her children, not disempowering them and their social skills and attitudes. Then if, as the child grows, they learn to welcome each individual they meet as just that, a unique individual with their own views and experiences, the mother, now in the spirit world, will feel less burdened by the restrictions she imposed on her family.

The following testimonial is from my time in The Midlands. Little did I know that what started as a routine healing session would see me travel to Turkey and then France to complete a client's deceased grandmother's wishes!

FAR AWAY IN AUSTRALIA

Monica

The first time I met Bríd was at a retirement party for our local Garda Síochána. We were sitting at the same table. After some small talk we got around to the subject of religion and the dead. We started to discuss spirits – a subject very close to my heart. I used to love listening to my grandparents and their neighbours telling stories of things that happened after a death. I really enjoyed Bríd's company and a great friendship followed.

Shortly after that evening I started to feel unwell. I met Bríd and, without telling her, she knew immediately that I needed help. She asked if I had twenty minutes to spare she would like to channel healing for me. I jumped at the invitation and went into a room with soft music playing. Bríd started the healing by praying and asked any spirits that could help me to come forth. I closed my eyes and left my troubles in Bríd's very capable hands. I relaxed for the first time in years.

I listened to the music on Bríd's DVD and recognised it as "Far away in Australia" my grandmothers favourite song. I felt heat on my eyes as they had been very sore and I felt completely rejuvenated after the healing session.

I mentioned to Bríd about the song on her DVD player. She said she had meant to change it before the healing session but forgot to do so. I told her it was meant to play as it was my grandmother's favourite song. When I went on holidays to her house as a child there was a record player and Grannie loved to listen to that song as some of her younger siblings went to Australia and never returned. They always kept in touch but never returned and two of them died in the First World War after they enlisted in the Australian Army. I knew it was my grandmother's way of letting me know she was there during the healing session, helping me. I left that day feeling like a new person and never looked back.

Afterwards I remembered the story of how two of my grandmother's brothers had gone to Australia as teenagers. They had an older brother there and he was able to get them work. However, some years later they both wanted to return to live in their native country but did not have the finances to start new lives at home. They decided to join the Anzac army and believed after a year they would be returning to Ireland. The brothers were separated: Joseph was placed in the war office in France and his younger brother Philip sent by ship to Turkey.

In 2011 my brother and his son went to visit the grave of our Grand-uncle Philip in Turkey. When he returned he told us the story and showed us all his photographs. My husband

and I decided that we would also visit the grave. We invited Bríd to come with us, not realising what we were letting her in for. On 22nd May 2012 we went on a coach tour of Gallipoli visiting three graveyards. Bríd was anxious the previous night. Going into a battlefield where all those young men had died was not going to be easy for her. As we approached the landings, Bríd passed us a prayer to keep saying. This was to help her cope and to help the young soldiers go to the light and to take this opportunity to cross over.

There were so many graveyards on that mountain as approximately one hundred and forty-seven thousand young men died there during the war. The coach stopped at the first graveyard and Bríd was drawn to the grave of a young soldier, a Maltese boy aged seventeen, who was possibly younger as they often lied about their age so they could enlist. Then she was drawn to the graves of two young English soldiers who left young wives and small children and then she was drawn to many more.

Our coach visited the beach of Sulva Bay where so many young men lost their lives while landing on the shore. The beach is overlooked by a mountain and the Turkish army was easily able to maintain their stronghold from such a vantage point. Bríd did a general crossing on the beach asking God to send healing to the land and help any souls who were willing to accept this opportunity to cross to the light.

We then proceeded on to the Irish graveyard. Again Bríd was mysteriously taken backwards, forwards, to the right and left. She crossed all she could in the short time we had there.

Then we continued to the graveyard "Lonepine" where my Grand-uncle Philip was buried.

We got off the coach and the rain poured down. We borrowed the guide's umbrella, I knew the Number and Row of the grave but I had no idea if it was to the right, left or straight ahead. I went right, then left and stopped; I looked around to see the other tourists getting back on the coach out of the rain. I worried I would not be able to find his grave so I called to Bríd not wanting to disturb her.

To my surprise Bríd told me there was no one approaching her for assistance in that graveyard as they knew we were Uncle Philip's visitors who travelled half way across the world to visit his grave, so no one interrupted us. I suddenly realised I was standing on the grave next to my Grand-uncle's, what a relief to have found it. Bríd and my husband stayed with me at the headstone while I buried a stone from the old fireplace of the house where Philip was born. This was something symbolic from the heart of his family home. Bríd reassured us he had already crossed. Thank God.

He explained to Bríd he held no grudge towards the Turkish army; his words were "The Turks got us fair and square." He also explained that his three months service on the ship were in fact the happiest time of his adult life as he thoroughly enjoyed the camaraderie shared with the other men. He expressed his gratitude for our visit. The fact it was raining heavily meant we were the only people in the graveyard. We could concentrate on our visit to him without being interrupted. The guide gave us extra time there as I was the only one on the coach to have a blood relative buried in Gallipoli.

Bríd asked her spirit guide that night how many soldiers she had helped cross over and the answer was more than forty and less than fifty. The following day she clearly showed the exhaustion incurred during so many crossings. We returned to Ireland with a sense of relief knowing that Philip was at peace.

In 2013 my husband, brother, nephew and I decided to make the trip to Normandy in France to visit the grave of our Grand-uncle Joseph (Philip's brother). Again we invited Bríd to accompany us. The night before we left Bríd stayed at our home. In the morning she relayed a vivid dream in which she had seen my grandmother (Joseph's sister), my father and an empty baby crib. Bríd said my grandmother had smiled at her and acknowledged her. Bríd said what was confusing her was the fireplace they were sitting at was at the opposite side of the room to our fireplace. I explained my parents had been living in a different house during the early years of their marriage.

We flew to Paris Beauvais on the 27th April 2013. My nephew had arranged car hire and drove us to the graveyard. Grand-uncle Joseph had died in a field hospital and had been buried in the accompanying graveyard. Similarly to the Dardanelles in Turkey, Bríd was called on by many souls for assistance. Finally we came to Joseph's grave. Bríd explained that he had not crossed over as he felt responsible for his brother's death. I remember my grandmother telling me that when Philip was killed in Turkey, Joseph, on hearing the news, asked to be removed from the war office and sent to the front line in retaliation for his brother's death.

This anger and the perceived responsibility for his brother's death had since prevented him moving forward. Bríd spoke with him and started saying her crossing prayers. As she did so she described my grandmother (who she recognised from her dream the previous night) standing with one man on her right with a moustache (presumably either her brother Philip, who died in Turkey, or their older brother John, who had invited them to go to Australia, as both had a moustache). On her left were six young men, all with their arms around each other. She described my grandmother stepping forward from the men with her arms outstretched to bring Joseph home to the light. Joseph had seven brothers, including Philip. It was very emotional for all of us. I buried a stone from the old fireplace of the house where he and Philip were born, and along with this I placed a stone from Sulva Bay where his younger brother had died and was buried.

I know my grandmother finally got her wish and is reunited with all her family.

When we returned to our hotel, Bríd offered to channel healing for my brother. A young girl appeared in spirit to Bríd, she said she was with us all day and was present at the cemetery. We recognised this girl as being our sister who died in infancy and was obviously happy to be present as Joseph was reunited with his family. It was possibly her cot that Bríd had observed in her dream the night before we left home to travel to France.

SPIRITS NOT GODS

"Never speak ill of the dead" is one of our Irish sayings. This is respectful, but just because someone has died, this does not automatically move them up the list for sainthood. My daily contact with the spirit world has shown me that our personalities and life stories do not change simply because we have died. If in this life we are a kind, loving and generous person then that will also be our personality when we pass on. Those whom we have loved and cared about while alive we will still love and care for when we are gone. If, however, we were uncaring, abusive, self-centred, and so on, in this life our deaths will not make us saints.

We all have people we go to when we are in trouble; someone who will listen to us and hopefully not judge us, offering a sympathetic ear (and lots of tea if you are Irish). We also have people that we would never even consider going to with our problems and concerns. Our reasons for choosing our advisors should remain the same when we are getting messages from those who are deceased. If, for example, Auntie was a kind, loving aunt who always had our best interest at heart, then yes we will take on board her words when she is gone.

However, if that aunt was always meddling, interfering, criticising, and always putting her needs before everyone else, then we should make up our own minds on any messages she may now have to pass on. Also we should remember that our aunt is now in spirit world, where she is just that, a spirit. She is not an angel or a God so interceding to her for world peace will have limited success. If she was someone who cared for you she will always care for you and will be with you in times of difficulty and will intercede for you when she can.

When I channel healing I invite in from the spirit world those who the client has lost. But I always make it clear that those I am inviting in are the spirits that are now with God. I am not opening a doorway for spirits on a lower vibration to join us as these spirits still have a long way to go in their own transitions in the spirit world. For example if Daddy was a kind and loving father, that's great, we would love to have him contribute to the healing session. However if he was abusive, or an addict, or had played no part in our lives then we do not need to allow him a stage to continue his old ways.

I ask clients, when possible, not to tell me before the session why they have come. I prefer it this way as I am not concentrating on any one issue or area. The healing then goes to wherever the client most needs it. It can be physical healing, emotional healing or spiritual healing. Over the years a number of adults who have come to me for healing are survivors of sexual abuse. While channelling healing I am shown physical areas that the client is receiving healing for. I am also shown symbols that represent different issues the client may have. They cover a multitude of subjects and I have dedicated the next chapter to explaining how this works for me. One of the symbols that spirits have occasionally shown me identifies the client has been a victim of sexual abuse.

After the healing has finished I sit with the client and discuss what they experienced during the session and then I go through what I have been shown. It amazes and humbles me that these people feel they can trust me to confirm what I have been shown. In many cases I am the only person they have ever shared their harrowing story with.

The angels and spirits, who help with these sessions, work to surround their loved one in peace and love. Any messages they may have are kind, gentle and reassuring. If, however, I left the "floor open" to all spirits who wished to communicate with the client I could even allow the abuser the opportunity to try to justify their actions. I believe it is always important when asking spirits to intervene for us or to guide us or help us in any way that we ask for the assistance that we specify those spirits who are now with God to step forward and help us and not include those on a lower vibration who may still be working on their transition in the spirit world.

This is something that is really important to remember for anyone thinking of getting a reading done. Make sure the psychic you choose is only working with the higher good as you may get messages from spirits that do not have your best interests as their number one concern. I believe the use of items like Ouija boards allows a doorway for all spirits on all levels to enter your space and allows them power. Would you open your front door to all criminals, abusers, those who traffic children, drug dealers and so on and invite them in for a bit of fun? I don't think so. Yet those who "play" with Ouija boards are potentially opening this door. As long as there is light there is also dark. When society makes Ouija boards and the dark side sound like an evening's light entertainment we need to be aware of what we could potentially be dealing with.

The summer before last, Margaret (a friend of mine, who is also clairsentient) and I were driving to a training course. It was a nice day, unusually so for Ireland, and we were enjoying the drive and coastal views. Margaret suggested we call in to the school in a nearby town to get a feel for it and see if any souls there may need our help. The school was not familiar to me. Margaret explained that it had been an industrial school for young boys and had been run by a religious order. The school received a lasting notoriety through revelation of physical and sexual abuse of the boys by some members of the order, with evidence of sexual abuse and extreme physical punishments going back over fifty years. It is believed that dozens of children died there while in the care of the order, many from abuse and neglect.

Some of the children there had been voluntarily admitted by parents or guardians as they simply could not afford to take care of them. More children were taken from unwed mothers or widowed fathers. Others were taken if they had been found breaking the law: something as simple as stealing an apple could result in a child being separated from his family.

On hearing the stories about the place, I agreed, thinking it would be a good thing to do to help cross over any young boys that had become trapped spirits there. Half an hour later we pulled into the car park. It was midterm so even though the school is still being used there was no one about. Not wanting to draw attention to ourselves or our mission I lit a tea light in the car and put it discreetly on the space by the handbrake. I grounded myself and said some prayers asking for protection. I asked those in spirit now with God who had loved ones trapped in this dimension at the school to come forward and help.

I got out of the car and walked around the area. I had so many emotions and symptoms being shown to me that it was overwhelming. The biggest shock I got was that those coming forward wanting to now cross to the light were not the children but some of their abusers. I stopped in my tracks not knowing what to do. In normal every day life these were not the people I would go out of my way to help. I asked my guides to intervene.

They explained to me that these abusers had come into this life with unblemished souls the same as we all do. Some may have been paedophiles when they joined the order. Others had not personally made the choice to join a religious order; this decision had been made for them by their parents and local clergy. Some had themselves been abused from a young age and gone on to become abusers. They were scared, frustrated and angry at the cards life had dealt them. They continued the circle of abuse, taking advantage of these innocent, traumatised boys that were placed in their care. When their time came to die and pass to the light the same religious beliefs that they at times resented stopped them from crossing. They believed that God would not forgive them and they would now burn in hell.

When I had started the prayers their loved ones in spirit came to help them home to the light. Some of their deceased parents carried huge guilt and regret for the decisions they had made to force their children into religious orders that had ended with such devastating consequences. These men's spirits needed to cross to the light so they could begin the journey of addressing their own actions.

Looking back at the car I noticed the tea light I had discretely lit now resembled an inferno and Margaret went to see if the car was on fire. She blew out the candle but now, instead of a huge flame, the car was encircled in smoke. I calmed myself and continued to pray with these men so they could commence their journey.

I could see in my mind's eye young boys coming forward but then hiding at the side of the building. They wanted to cross but there was no way they were going anywhere their abusers were going. The children questioned me as to why, if these men, who abused them were God's representatives, these children would want to meet this God. I explained that God loves all His children. This does not mean we can do whatever we like and abuse others. When we cross over we have to account for our actions, as would these men.

I tried to encourage the children to come forward, but they refused. I promised to return to the school at a later date. I then saw the spirits of three young boys hiding in the back of our car. They had decided to trust us to get them out of there. But they were going to leave by car and not cross to the light with their abusers.

I got back in the car and spoke encouraging words to the boys (and also to Margaret who really was not sure about taking three young spirits for a drive). I told them we meant them no harm. I explained that the things they had endured had not been their fault. They had done nothing wrong. I told them about the God of my understanding and of His love for them. He does not approve of what had been done to these children, and especially by people taking His name. I told them about their parents and siblings desperately waiting for them to come home to the light. That their parents were unable to prevent the state taking their children and how their crossing would bring so much peace to their own families who were waiting to be united with them.

I have found that while I am carrying out a crossing that if someone (living) is assisting me they may feel the symptoms of the trapped spirit as this seems the easiest way for the spirit to communicate. Also it is generally less frightening for the person assisting me to briefly feel a pain than to see a trapped spirit.

We left the school and drove to a nearby beach. On the way Margaret and I could feel pressure on our kidneys. We could also feel punches to our sides and slaps across the face. I was then shown pictures in my mind's eye of how the boys would not be allowed to the bathroom during the school day, which would result in pains in their kidneys and with them eventually wetting themselves. They would then get a beating for this. When they went to wash and change, some of the children were then assaulted. I again reassured them.

On reaching the beach I lit a tea light and asked their loved ones to come forward. I could feel myself surrounded in complete love. I could feel the tears of joy from both the parents and the three young boys. I wished them well and said goodbye. That night the child who had been the bravest of the three came to me in my dreams. I could see his freckles and his bowl cut hairstyle. He was smiling and had beautiful dimples. He told me his name was Alan and that he and his friends were safe and had been reunited with their families. He thanked me and was gone.

The following summer Margaret and I again returned to the school. I had been hoping that this time it would only be the boys that we would encounter. I know my spirit guide had explained that the men also needed help but if possible I didn't want to be the one helping them.

This time it was just the boys. They came forward in little groups. One little boy, who looked to be about six years old would not cross to the light without first showing me the details of his abuse and the unspeakable circumstances of his death. He needed to share these details before he could find peace. I cried as he showed me his last moments of life, but then felt the tears of joy at seeing his parents come to bring him back to the light.

I must stress that it is very unusual for anyone who dies as a child not to pass immediately to the light. These children I met had chosen not to cross originally for various reasons. Some had promised to take care of younger siblings, and felt they could not leave. Some had felt responsible for their new friends. Others believed the promises of their parents that they would come and get them back and so they had remained to wait. While more of the children didn't want to go to the God of their abusers. By the time I came to do a crossing with them their parents and loved ones had already died. These deceased relatives were now finally able to keep their promises to their children by now coming forward to bring them home.

SIGNS & SYMBOLS

There is another Irish saying: "People die twice, once when their heart stops beating and once when their name is uttered for the last time." If you have loved ones who have passed on, don't be afraid to chat with them the same as you always have, though maybe not in public! Keep the connection alive.

I had a friend, Mary, around for breakfast this morning while I was writing this chapter. She had taken the day off work as twenty-one years ago today she had a miscarriage. It had been a boy whom she had named Thomas. She was taking the day off to spend with him and to celebrate their connection. I thought it was a beautiful thing to do for both of them.

A lot of people find comfort visiting their loved ones' grave. But we can connect with spirit from anywhere – whether it's sitting in our kitchen, walking on the beach or driving to work. We can chat out loud as normal or have the conversations in our heads. They will be delighted to hear from us and to know that they are remembered. If we are open and receptive the spirit world and our angels will give us signs or proof of their presence. This is never meant to scare us and is gentle and loving.

Finding a white feather is a well documented evidence that our guardian angel is with us. Sometimes a song will come on the radio just as we turn it on with a reference to an angel. You may be worried about how a personal situation will get solved as you turn on your radio in time to hear "In the arms of an angel." You may be thinking of a deceased loved one when a song they used to sing or dance to will come on the radio like the story "Far away in Australia".

Sometimes we may find tears coming from one of our eyes for no apparent reason, this can also be evidence that our angels are near us. A client, Kate, this week told me how she had recently been at a family event and was finding the whole occasion very difficult. She asked Archangel Michael to stand beside her and give her strength. Almost immediately she noticed tears coming from her left eye. She believed Archangel Michael had heard her prayers and was letting her know he was now standing beside her as requested.

Occasionally we may smell a familiar fragrance or perfume of a deceased loved one. One evening I was expecting two female clients. I had got my treatment room ready, heat on, candles lit, music playing softly; it all felt very peaceful. About ten minutes before the clients were due I went to check that I had everything in the room that I might need. I was shocked by the smell or should I say stench that greeted me. I could not work out where it came from. I looked under the couch, and behind furniture, thinking the dog must have brought in something.

I could not solve it and by now the women were due so I couldn't cancel. With that the doorbell went. The first of the two women entered the treatment room. I apologised for the terrible smell, which reminded me of gutted fish. With that she started crying. When she finally composed herself she explained that the last time she had seen her father alive they had gone fishing together and he had got her to gut the fish. With that the smell disappeared and she had received absolute proof that her dad was in the spirit world and very much still with her.

We can also learn from the animals that enter and exit our lives. By studying these animals and their characteristics we can apply this to our own lives and see what lessons nature is trying to help us with. These can be animals we actually see: a stray dog or cat, a rabbit or fox, spiders, birds, fish. We can also have dreams about animals and when I am doing healing I am often shown animals as totems for the client.

Many people spend their lives studying the relationships between humans and animals, believing that the animals in our lives offer us guidance and support once we take notice and understand their significance. There are many published books and cards on animals and nature and their significance in our lives.

During a past relationship I dreamt I was out with my partner looking at properties and we had our dog with us. But in the dream our dog changed into a crocodile on a lead being led around by my partner. The first reference I thought of the next morning was crocodile tears suggesting that my partner was not being truthful, which immediately put me on my guard. Crocodiles also represent birth and motherhood as they are excellent mothers and can lay up to sixty eggs which she gently and protectively takes care of. I took this as a sign that a new stage in my life was about to begin (birth).

Dogs represent the pack and faithfulness yet the dog had disappeared to be replaced by a crocodile. Later that week my partner (whom I had in reality started looking at properties with) told me he had decided to move to a property on his own and that he no longer wished to be with me. (I got the whole, "It's not you, it's me" speech.) Thankfully the dream had gone some way towards preparing me and also gave me some encouragement to move forward as a new stage in my life was going to open up.

When animal totems started showing up during healing sessions at first I had no idea what was going on. The first time this happened it was a mouse I could see in my mind's eye. I chose not to pass this piece of information on to the client as I decided saying "I can see a mouse!" probably wouldn't have benefited her healing process. It was some weeks later when discussing this with a friend that they explained the significance of animals and animal totems to me. I treated myself to some books on animals and their totems. The first one I looked up was the mouse. Mice tend to have poor vision in sunlight so the universe may be trying to tell you to be more observant of what is going on around you. When I think of mice I think of Jerry in the cartoons living in the little hole in the corner. If a mouse has come as a totem maybe it is time to move out of our home more often and experience the world around us, instead of just going out to do the necessities of getting food and supplies and so on, before returning to the safety of our home.

Shortly afterwards when a camel appeared during a healing session I took the vision in my stride (not literally) and was able to talk to the client about her tendency of storing things up and the need to let go. We looked at her habit of carrying the burdens of others. Camels can also be an indication of travel, be it a holiday or a love of travelling and exploring new terrains. The image of the camel was a huge help as it showed the topics we needed to explore and discuss as part of her healing session.

On one occasion during a healing session I could see a donkey. Afterwards, while chatting with the client, I explained all about animals and animal totems and their significance. I then told her that during her session I had been shown a donkey with a red collar standing by a low wall with a metal gate. I went on to talk about possible significances like travel and issues around freedom. None of this meant anything to the client but finally she told me that as a young child her family had a donkey with a red collar that used to wait by the gate for her after school. Sometimes when I see an animal that is exactly what the message is, someone is showing me a memory of a pet animal that was significant to them at some point in their life. The challenge for me is to know when it is a memory and when it is a totem animal.

A female client, Eimear came to see me one evening. The session started the same as most healing sessions do. I placed my hands near the client's head where there is always healing needed for all the stress we carry. Then I could see her mother who is in the spirit world sitting on a stool beside her daughter, Eimear, reading a novel, while every so often lovingly glancing over at the daughter. I could see lots of green light going to Eimear's heart for emotional healing so I moved around to stand by her side. As I did so I was confronted by a cow. Its face was so close to mine that I jumped back with fright. It put out its tongue and I thought it was going to lick my face. I was so relieved to remind myself that this cow was not actually in my treatment room. I am still not sure who spoke, whether it was Eimear's mother or the cow, but someone said "Bluee". I acknowledged Bluee the cow, who then promptly disappeared and I continued channelling healing for Eimear.

Afterwards we sat to chat through what had come up during the session. I told her about her mum, and Eimear told me her mum always loved to read and would always have a book on the go. I then told her about Bluee and Eimear started to cry, real heart wrenching sobs which startled me as I had no idea how significant Bluee was to Eimear.

Eimear explained, through the tears, that she was from a small remote rural farm, where she lived with her parents and her brother, who had health problems. Eimear's childhood friends were her father's cows whom she had given names to. She especially loved Bluee who would walk up to her and lick her. One summer Eimear's brother had become very ill and had gone into hospital. Eimear's mother had gone to stay with a relative who lived near the hospital, leaving Eimear and her father to take care of their home and farm.

All cattle in Ireland are annually tested. Their animals failed the test that summer and had to be taken away and put down. Eimear was devastated. She described the event from some forty years ago. Her father called her early in the morning to help him put in all the cattle and have them ready for the lorry. He was trying not to cry. The lorry driver, feeling sorry for Eimear, went to give her a pound, a lot of money to a child in those times. Eimear refused to take the coin wanting no reward for this terrible event. The cattle, including her favourite and beloved Bluee, were loaded up and driven away.

Her father broke down crying, leaving Eimear, who was about nine years old at the time, feeling responsible for his care.

He was now a farmer with no animals, his son was seriously ill in hospital and his wife was gone to care for him. He was devastated. Eimear felt she should not cry as this would only add to her father's misery.

Since that day Eimear had carried that hurt, the loss of her friend Bluee, and the sense of responsibility as caretaker for her father. In her adult life she continued to find herself in relationships as the caretaker. She was the giver, the responsible one. Her needs always took second place. I believe the healing she received that evening, along with the pain she released from her heart helped not just her to heal but also her parents in the spirit world who felt guilty for the responsibility placed on their child and the impact the events of that summer had on her life.

Occasionally our guides, angels, loved ones in spirit try to communicate with us through our dreams. These dreams can be a scene by scene copy of an event we are about to encounter. This type of dream tends to be as we are falling into sleep or waking from sleep. Symbolic dreams can be for a number of reasons: they can be to protect us, to let us know that they are aware of what is happening in our lives and trying to get us to pay more attention to our dreams or to other signs; and dreams can be confirmation that we are not alone. They can go some way in preparing us for difficult events and challenges. Some factual dreams can help us alter events. For example if we dream of a family member in an accident, we can remind them to drive with care and wear their safety belt, and avoid using their mobile and so on.

Most dreams seem to come in code and we have to work at deciphering them. If we go back to my dream of my partner walking a crocodile on a lead instead of our dog, after waking up I was sure we were not about to purchase a crocodile so I had to look deeper for a meaning. Then, when I thought about crocodile tears, I knew this was a warning that my partner was not being honest with me.

A lot of symbols in dreams mean the opposite of what we see in the dream. In my dream, last night, I and some friends were among a large convoy of trucks on our way to join a war. Thankfully, contrary to what you would immediately assume, war in a dream symbolises peace, happiness and friendship. Similarly, dreams about births tend to represent a forthcoming death and vice versa when we dream of a death it can signify a birth. In a recent dream I was in a maternity hospital after a baby boy was born. My brother was also in the dream. He stepped forward and offered to take care of the baby. The next day we learnt that a bachelor who lived near us and who had in his youth worked on our family farm had died unexpectedly of a heart attack. My brother helped with arrangements and the digging of the grave.

I had a very vivid dream when I was starting practising spiritual healing. In the dream it was a lovely sunny day. I was lying on the lawn and I was barefoot. A bee flew over head. I held up my foot and it landed on my big toe. Soon another bee came and landed beside it. One at a time, more and more bees gradually landed on me. My foot now resembled a bee hive and still they continued to swarm up along my leg, one at a time. Strangely I was not afraid and continued holding up my leg for them to land on. I could feel some of them but they did not sting, if anything it tickled.

On waking the next morning I thought what a strange dream and put some thought into deciphering it. I took this to be a really good omen that my business would prove to be very successful. When I reflected on the way the bees came one at a time I took it that this is also how my clients would come. My reputation would build up gradually and spread by word of mouth. One bee would follow another. And so it is today, I have never placed an advertisement for my services yet somehow my clients learn of my gift from clients that have already been to see me.

The more detail we can remember from our dreams the more information we will be able to collate. For example, if we are on a boat or ship and the sailing is smooth this signifies a contented family life whereas if there is a stormy sea it is an indication of impending arguments or being unhappy. There are lots of books to be found on the subject of dreams and we can also find explanations on the internet. Sometimes different books will give different meanings. I believe the relevant significance will be whatever reference book or belief you have about dream meanings. If the dream is being used as a conduit for passing on information it will be in line with our beliefs of their meanings and the information we have available to us at that time.

Another documented way for angels to communicate with us is through number sequences. These sequences could be on a clock, car mileage, licence plates, invoices, bar code, and so on. You may look at the time 3.33; then your mileage clock will turn to 72333; and the car in front of you has 333 as part of their car registration. If you do notice these numbers reoccurring you could look at the significance of number sequences. Do pay attention and then it is up to you: do you just write it off as a strange coincidence, or is there a message your angels are trying to bring to your attention?

A young woman came to see me recently. She admitted that she had been considering suicide. In the depths of despair she was surprised by the fact that she kept seeing the number 3 repeated constantly. At first this meant nothing to her but with growing repetition of the number she decided to do some research into number sequences. She was amazed to discover this was a well documented phenomenon and that seeing 3's indicated that the Ascended Masters are close by and interceding on your behalf.

In brief terms my understanding of number sequences and their meanings are as follows:

000 – You are one with the Creator. We are reminded of divine love. The 000 can also show us that something we have been working towards, or praying for has finally come full circle.

111 – Pay attention to what your thoughts are at the moment, making sure you are only focusing on what you want. The universe has chosen this moment to give you what it is you are thinking about.

222 – You have almost achieved one of your ambitions; keep up the good work; you have got a bit more work to do before it becomes reality for you.

333 – The Ascended Masters are especially near you at this moment in time; ask them for help with what ever is bothering you or what you are striving towards. If it is in your best interest and the right time they will help you with your task in hand. If you are feeling alone, know that they are with you.

444 – This is similar to 333 except, instead of the Ascended Masters being near you, it is your angels that have drawn especially close to you at this time. If there is something important that you are working on they are showing you 444 to show their approval and that they will help where possible. Pay attention and know you are not alone.

555 – There is about to be a major positive change in your life. You are being shown the numbers so you will be ready to embrace the change or opportunity when it is presented to you.

666 – You need to bring balance back into your life. Are you putting too much focus on one aspect of your life, be that work, material gain, or personal achievement?

777 – Well done, congratulations, keep up the good work. So if you have taken up meditation, exercise, de-cluttering, self improvement in any form or starting a new venture you may be getting 777 on car registrations, food wrappers, bar codes, invoices, and so on.

888 – Something that is important to you is about to come to an end. It may be a job, relationship, friendship. But this needs to happen for you to move forward and although it may be painful while you are going through the change, the 888 is to comfort you and to encourage you to keep going. The pain will pass and a new and brighter chapter is about to open up for you.

999 – Something you have been working on is about to reach completion. It could be something that you have been praying for for a very long time, almost to the point of giving up. Your prayers have been heard but could not be granted before now because of divine timing.

The number sequence can be unique to the individual, their house number, the day of the month they or their first child was born, the anniversary of a loved one. The most common number sequences for me are 44 and 444. Frequently when I have to travel to do my healing work I will see this combination on the number-plate of the car travelling in front of me, or the time of arrival at my destination with often include 44.

Sometimes before a healing session I can feel overwhelmed by the severity of the client's illness or the enormity of their burdens and question myself if I am up to the task. Seeing a number sequence like 11:44 reminds me that I am not the one doing the healing; I am just the channel; my angels and those of the client are present. The 11 reminds me to focus my thoughts and remain positive. Seeing 111 reminds me to stay focused on the task in hand.

LEARNING TO LET GO

The connections we have while alive will continue always. As we progress here in this lifetime, our loved ones progress in the next world. Often during healing sessions the messages from the deceased help the living, which in turn can help the deceased deal with some of their outstanding issues.

Christmas 2011, I was channelling healing for a female client. I could see so many spirits coming in to help. Most of these appeared to be sitting in a day room like you would find in a hospice or old folks' home. I explained this to the client and she said that she volunteers at a hospice. I could see the first spirit in the day room exceptionally clearly and she was the only one who spoke. Her message was very brief: "I am OK, I really am OK!"

I described this woman to the client and the clothes she was wearing. The client immediately knew this was her mother, whom she had also nursed at the hospice. The clothes I described were the clothes the daughter had chosen to lay her mother out in for her funeral. She took this as real evidence that her mother was now in the next world.

I then asked her about her mother's words "I am OK, I really am OK!" Again the daughter explained that for some months before her mother's death she had had many hallucinations as a result of the medication she was on. The daughter had spent much of this time reassuring her mother: "you will be OK, you really will be OK".

After her mother's death, however, she had often wondered whether her mother was actually OK and whether she was now at peace. Her mother's words brought her enormous reassurance and she was able to stop worrying. This also helped her mother now in the spirit world as she knew her fears caused by the hallucinations had impacted on her daughter. The daughter was now able to let this go and at the same time her mother could let it go and both could now progress and moved forward together.

Not all spirits wait until their loved ones have arrived at my home for treatments before they try to communicate with me. Occasionally spirits can approach me for various reasons at any point of the day. Thankfully this does not happen too often.

Now when I pick up on someone else's pain or sadness I acknowledge it as that of someone else. I ask for healing and love for that person or situation, then I thank God and the angels for the healing sent and leave the spirit in their care. I then release myself from that pain. It sounds quite straightforward but sometimes it takes me a while to realise the pain is not mine.

When I was quite new to working with spirit I woke one morning with intense tooth ache. I phoned up the dentist and asked for an emergency appointment as the toothache was so bad. The dentist agreed to see me straight away. On examination he explained that I did not have a tooth in the area I was experiencing the pain. I realised that it was someone in spirit trying to get my attention. I paid the dentist and left. Once safely back in my car I invited the spirit to come forward and to explain what message was so important as to cause me such pain and embarrassment. This spirit was the father of a close friend and was worried about his daughter. He asked for a message to be passed on to her immediately.

Because my strongest gift is that I am clairsentient I do not always see the spirits when they are trying to communicate with me. Instead I feel their symptoms. When I know a spirit is trying to connect with me I pray for the spirit and I then wash my hands. I say something like "thank you for showing me this situation (name the situation) and for the healing and love sent; I now release myself from this situation and return this spirit to God's care". If I am not near water I have learnt that I can disconnect from the spirit by wiping my hands on my clothes or just by rubbing my hands together, saying thanks and asking to be released.

The method used really does not matter. It is the intention, the belief in the prayers and the expression of gratitude that get the results.

Some years back I was a passenger in a car coming back home after a holiday on the south coast of Ireland. As we went around a turn in the road I felt the sensation of my neck break. Because of the fact that my strongest gift is that I am clairsentient, the easiest way for spirit to communicate is by transferring their symptoms at time of death onto me, and this is exactly what had just happened. I realised someone had broken their neck in a car incident and died there as a result of their injuries. They were now trying to get my attention for help. I asked the driver of our car to stop. We walked back to the area and discovered a plaque on the road side in memory of a man who had died there. I asked

God, my angels, archangels and guides for protection and asked those passed on to God who cared for this man to help. I spoke with this man's spirit and then said prayers with him to help him cross over, asking for a passage way to be opened for him.

The man's spirit showed me pictures in my mind's eye of where he had lived. He had got caught up in the "Celtic Tiger" and built a large home. He showed me a stack of unpaid bills indicating he was unable to meet his mortgage repayments and was not able to sustain his new lifestyle. He had believed suicide was his only way out and had decided to make it look like an accident. This he thought would ease the pain in the aftermath of his death for his family and loved ones. With an accidental death his life assurance would be paid out without complications or delays. This would clear his mortgage leaving his wife without that financial worry. Once he had decided on this plan of action he was totally convinced this was the right thing to do as he felt he had let everyone down when he lost his job, could no longer provide financially for his family and felt he no longer had a role to fill in life.

However, once he had gone through with his plan he was filled with regrets for the life he had cut short. He also carried huge remorse for the pain his actions had caused his loved ones. I chatted with this man's trapped spirit and reassured him that God loves us all. I asked the angels for a passage way to be opened for his soul and for his loved ones in spirit to come and help him on his journey. I then said the crossing prayers. Once done I thanked all those who had come to help and handed the man and his situation back to God.

At that stage I was pretty new to doing crossings. The ones I had performed prior to this were planned events with someone (living) coming to my home or phoning me asking for my assistance. On those occasions I had time to pray and to ground myself, and to equip myself with blessed salts, candles, and water and so on. This was different in that it was an unplanned event. On this occasion I did find a tea light candle in the glove compartment, but I did not have any water. I now know that the materials used for the crossing, the prayers said and the method used for disconnecting are not important; it is the intention that matters and the belief in what is happening. On the day in question I had not worked all that out yet so believed the only way I could disconnect from the trapped spirit and the crossing process was by washing my hands. The only water I could find at the road side was in a muddy puddle!

I have discovered that, even though a trapped soul may approach me for help, asking for a passage way to open for them and saying prayers with them is not always enough to enable their crossing. Occasionally I need to go through an additional process with them that I call cutting the cords.

Usually at this stage I will have identified the reason they have not crossed over and it will be fairly obvious which cord is still holding back the soul's progression. Like the following story "Memories & Missions". While in Nenagh, County Tipperary, I went to help two brothers who had been hung in the 1850s. After initially doing the prayers with them they had still not taken the opportunity to cross to the light. I realised it was the cord of injustice that was still holding them back. They could not accept that their young lives could be taken for a crime they had not committed and been in no way responsible for. But the authorities of the time had not seemed to care about discovering the truth. I asked Archangel Michael to help me cut this cord which still held these men here and I explained to the two men what I was doing. Once this was achieved I repeated the prayers to enable them to finally make their journey.

MEMORIES AND MISSIONS

Martin

Having been recently asked by Bríd to write something for a book that she intends to publish, I began to remember some of the experiences I've had with her. Bríd is far from ordinary, in fact she is extraordinary.

At some stage I heard she did some sort of healing and out of curiosity I booked a session with her. During the session which entailed me being brought to her treatment room, taking off my shoes and lying on a treatment couch. Bríd began by saying some prayers and asking all and sundry including my guardian angel, Archangel Michael, my ancestors and a host of other entities to come to my aid during the healing. After some time she said she could see a cottage, tiny, maybe only one room with the only furniture being a rough hewn table with an apple tart freshly made and an elderly woman, grandmother, maybe great grandmother having it made for me. The name of the place was Killary.

Later Bríd asked me what the unusual smell was. I became aware of it and recognised it as the distinctive smell of my grandmother's room. It brought memories flooding back as only a scent memory can. My grandmother's grandparents originated from Killary almost two hundred years ago.

Subsequently, on occasion, Bríd would ask me to drive her to some part of the country, having injured her leg on some furniture manoeuvre or her car not functioning. I became her chauffeur on a few missions, whose purpose I'm not at liberty to state here; for one reason or another, confidentiality was requested.

One fine evening we were to rendezvous with some people in Nenagh. Being a little early and having seen the old jail, (now a convent) the thought entered my mind that I would put Bríd to the test. I stopped outside the Convent of Mercy in the town and pointed to the arch at the entrance. I asked her: "Do you see that arch there, do you feel anything?" Her answer was "I'm hanging." She had no way of knowing that the archway was once the old entrance to the jail where two brothers, on 11 May 1858 had been hung from a scaffold at that archway for a crime they did not commit.

Sometimes it won't be as obvious to me which cord is holding the soul back and preventing their progress. Even in death souls still retain their personalities. If someone was shy or timid, or maybe during their life did not believe in "this sort or thing" they may not be forthcoming to me regarding the circumstances of their deaths. In these instances I have again asked Archangel Michael to assist me and have gone through the alphabet until I find the cord that is holding back the soul's progression. I have asked for the cords of **a**nger, **b**itterness, cruelty, deceit, evil, fear, greed, and so on until I find the problem. Thankfully this has not happened to me too often.

Some months after my encounter with these two brothers I visited friends in Tipperary. I told them the story of my meeting with the two brothers who had been hung in Nenagh. I explained that it had proven very difficult for me to cut the cord of injustice which had prevented the younger brother from crossing to the light and that his older brother, feeling responsible for his sibling, had refused at the time of death to go without him. As faith would have it, one of my friends knew the history of the men and knew that they had been buried in Loughmore. She offered to drive me there to see the monument that is erected in their memory. Here she recollects the events of the day.

LOUGHMORE

Monica

One weekend Brid came to visit. While she was at our house she told us about her recent encounters with the spirit world, including her story about the McCormack brothers who had been executed in Nenagh for a crime they had not been guilty of. I offered to go with her to their graveyard, some twenty miles away. Brid agreed; my daughter also decided to come, so she drove. When we got near the little village, there was a crossroads, with no sign post, we decided to go left. We travelled on for 2 klm then we stopped at another cross roads again with no signpost. Eventually a jeep came by and the driver enquired if we needed directions. We had to return to the village by a different road making a full circle back.

On our way back I was sitting in the back of the car and as we crossed over a bridge I began to feel very sick, my head started to pain me really bad and I felt like I wanted to get sick. At that Brid asked my daughter to stop the car, as she felt very ill; she said she felt the symptoms of a pregnant spirit. We slowly drove up to the village and as we got to the gates of the graveyard Brid started to speak to someone invisible to me. As we drove into the church grounds the graves were all around us and Brid continued to pray out loud and said we have a young girl's spirit in the car with us who is looking for help. Brid got out of the car and seemed to follow some unseen guide, she eventually sat at the side of an old broken headstone and continued to speak to this spirit.

I got out of the car as I felt so ill now and I needed fresh air. My daughter (who did not feel any unusual symptoms) joined Brid and after about ten minutes I suddenly felt better and all my sickness had left me. I realised that at that moment the poor girl had just crossed to the light and left all her woes behind.

I joined the girls to ask what had happened. Brid told me she had crossed a young girl's spirit to the light. The girl had told Brid that she had got work as a live-in housekeeper and became pregnant by the nephew of her employer back in the 1800s. The spirit told Brid her name, Lizzy, and that she was sixteen, and told her how she died. She said it was considered such a shame, the family of the father of the unborn child had arranged for her to be taken out at night and drowned her in the river. They buried her in a freshly made grave, so no one would find her. An elderly man had been buried there the day before. Her family had been told she had run away.

Her final resting place was beside that of the McCormack brothers whom we had originally set out to pray for that day.

It is Brid's belief that there are no coincidences and we were meant to help Lizzy that day, and that the McCormack brothers would have wanted her to be assisted to cross to the light. We realised we took the long way round to the graveyard to share her last journey with her and when we crossed the bridge that was where she was drowned. She could not cross over because the cord of injustice done to her and her unborn child needed to be severed.

Throughout our lifetime we all accumulate issues and blocks that we find hard to release. We do not have to wait until we die to cut these cords. Once we acknowledge honestly to ourselves what our issue is we can start working on releasing it. There are a number of self-help books, CDs and meditations available to help us deal with the issues we encounter now.

There is similar material available to us to help cut the cords, which link us to unhealthy or co-dependent relationships with partners, family members, friendships and work colleagues that hold us back during our lives. The more work we can do on ourselves now the less we will have to do when it comes our turn to pass on. My choice of the word "work" may not be the best. If we see it as work or a chore we may be limiting ourselves. If we can approach this with a sense of joy and achievement we will get a lot more out of these exercises.

The following is a short meditation on cutting cords. It can be performed with a group or on your own. The intention being to cut cords that binds us in an unhealthy manner to present or past relationships. Weather permitting you may find it more beneficial to do outside in nature.

EXERCISE
RELEASING UNHEALTHY CORDS

Find a peaceful space where you will not be disturbed and play some gentle background music. If more than one person is present appoint a facilitator to read. Sit comfortably in a circle. If you are on your own, picture yourself among a small circle of your closest friends whom you trust and feel completely safe with. In the stillness say some prayers, mantras or affirmations for healing for all participants.

Sit quietly for a few minutes concentrating on your breathing. Become aware of your whole body and allow your attention to pass from the top of your head all the way down to your feet. Observe any tensions held in the body. Breathe deeply, visualising your breath moving into those parts of your body where the tension is held and picture the tension being released on the out breath. Continue this breathing exercise until fully relaxed.

Visualise the circle surrounded in golden light protecting you, the other participants and the intention of this process. Know that you are safe and protected.

Ask yourself with whom you need to cut any unhealthy cords. In the quietness of your mind explain in your own words to this person why you have chosen to cut these unhealthy binds and that by doing so you are allowing any ties remaining to be based in love and mutual respect for each other. This will be of mutual benefit to both of you, allowing each of you to move forward without control or domination by the other party, allowing all past perceived hurts to be released.

Visualise that person now entering the centre of the circle. Scan their body and your own to see where in your bodies the cords are connected. What is binding you together? Feel the texture? Is it made from thread, wire, rope, or chain? Does it have locks, or weights? How tight are the knots? Again scan your body; do you feel any tensions, tightness, pain or other sensation anywhere in your body?

Choose the tool needed to cut the connection. Use as much force as necessary. If you need assistance ask Archangel Michael (The archangel of protection) to help with his sword.

Imagine a log campfire burning to your right, it is surrounded by stones and is quite safe. Now pick up all the broken pieces of the cord and place them in the campfire. Make sure all the pieces are in the fire. Take a moment to watch them burn.

Scan your body again to see if it requires healing to the areas where the binds have been removed from. Place your hands over these areas and invite Archangel Raphael (the archangel of healing) to fill the void with healing love.

Now scan the body of the person you have severed the unhealthy cords with. Do they need healing? Again invite Archangel Raphael to fill these voids with healing love.

Thank Archangel Michael and Archangel Raphael for their assistance. Thank the person with whom you have cut all cords for helping you to learn these painful life lessons. Ask for their forgiveness for anything you may have done to hurt them. If it feels appropriate to do so imagine both of you embracing each other. Now allow them to move out of the circle.

Sit quietly in the golden circle. Become aware of your whole body and allow your attention to pass from the top of your head all the way down to your feet. Observe any tensions held in the body. Breathe deeply, visualising your breath moving into those parts of your body where the tension is held and picture the tension being released on the out breath.

Now it is time to come back to conscious awareness. When you are ready, open your eyes and take a few moments to readjust to the light and to your surroundings.

SUICIDE

This book would not be complete without writing down some of my thoughts on suicide. I have met so many people deeply affected by the loss of a loved one by their own hand. I have also met a number of trapped spirits who died as the result of suicide and then felt they could not move on to the light because of their actions.

In the past the Catholic Church in Ireland, has taken a very strong stance on suicide. It stated that suicide was a mortal sin that God would not forgive. In our not too distant history, anyone who committed suicide could not be buried in consecrated ground and therefore bodies were not buried in their family plots with other family members. There was a huge stigma associated with suicide. This added a lot of additional distress to the family of the deceased. Now thankfully this is no longer the teachings of the Church and family members can be buried together, though sadly there is still a stigma that goes with this type of death.

Often I am asked, "Why is it that people take their own life?" The reasons are as numerous as the people who commit suicide. It can be as a result of an acute event with detrimental consequences or due to depression, addiction, ill health, broken relationships, fear, low self-esteem, financial worry, stress about exams, unemployment – sadly, the list of reasons goes on.

At the time of their death, many believed (at that moment in time) that their death would end their suffering and frequently believed that their death would make it better for those left behind. I believe that God loves all of his children equally. On rare occasions when during the act of suicide the soul may have felt guilt, regret, sorrow, possibly even believing the Catholic Church's old teachings that God would not forgive them. At the time of their death, their loved ones in spirit came to bring them home, yet because of their individual beliefs and circumstances some may have chosen not to go with their loved ones to the light. I am by no means saying that everyone who chooses to end their own life will not cross immediately to the light, but I have found that this does seem to be one of the reasons that can hold a soul back from progressing.

From my experience, trapped souls are those who have, by their own decision, chosen not to go to the light at the time of their death. Instead, they continue to spend their time on our earthly plain. For these trapped souls their pains, fears and regrets remain. Their movement is more cumbersome, they are weighed down, similar to wearing a heavy full-length overcoat on a very sunny day. Their souls have now left their human bodies and their soul is fighting against gravity. Their death has not improved their situation and they are confused and lost.

When a lost soul gets my attention I tune in and try to work out what their individual situation is. Every trapped soul has a unique story. Once I have this information I reassure them that God is unconditional love and therefore loves all of us equally and is more than happy to welcome all of us home. I then pray, asking for another passageway to be made available to the trapped soul and I ask their guides and loved ones to come close and bring this troubled soul home.

What of those that do take their opportunity to pass on to the light? Once they have crossed over, their earthly pains and illnesses will cease, be that depression, stress, tension, physical disabilities and all disease. But their soul will still have the same essence. Those they have loved and cared for will still hold the same significance. Their memories will remain.

Situations that existed before their death will probably remain unchanged. For example, if they had injured someone in a car accident while drunk driving that person will still have the same injuries. If they owed someone money, that person will still carry that financial loss. If they had an argument with a loved one, the words spoken in the heat of the moment will go unaltered. Their death can not change or undo the past and now that the person is deceased they are no longer in a position to improve the situation. They can not apologise to a loved one that they may feel they have wronged. They will never learn to stand up to the bully in their life. They can no longer work to rebuild a relationship. They can not pay off a debt. They can play no further physical role in this lifetime. They can only watch from the wings. Suicide is not a quick fix solution, yet prior to their death, in their despair, it may appear that way.

There are lots of theories on what happens when one passes to the light. I believe that no one passes alone. When it is our time to leave we make the journey home in the company of our loved ones who have gone before us. From what I have been shown it would appear that at least two loved ones who have gone before us will come to reassure us and to escort us home to the light. Our guides who have been assigned to us all our lives now lovingly help us to reflect on the life we have lived. These guides help us to review what we have done and what we have not done during our time on earth. Also with their help we are able to reflect on the lives that we have touched both positively and negatively, the actions we have to account for, the positives and negatives of our lives. This allows us the opportunity to work through our issues, to address whatever negative karma we have accumulated and to learn from it.

When someone commits suicide their soul can occasionally carry regret and remorse with them. After their death they are in a position to watch their loved ones trying to come to terms with their loss. Frequently those left behind feel near breaking point; with the circumstances surrounding the death, and possibly with guilt that they somehow had not prevented the event. When those left behind start to put their lives back together and move forward again, this in turn helps their deceased loved one to more forward, bringing spiritual healing to both the living and to the dead.

A woman in her mid-twenties came to see me. There was such a terrible sadness with her. During her healing session a teenage boy communicated with us. He was her brother and had died at his own hand. He explained that he had been drinking and did not think his actions on that fateful night would actually result in his death. He thought he would be found in time, brought to the hospital and his family and friends would all come and fuss over him. He was really shocked when he realised he was dead.

He told her he loved her and called her by his pet name for her. He told her not to worry, that he was fine. He said he was now allowed to drive unaccompanied on that side. While alive he was still on a provisional licence and had to be accompanied by a qualified driver. He used to always complain that he was a good driver and didn't need someone with him. The woman took this evidence as confirmation that the message was real. It was of huge comfort to the young woman and in turn lessened his guilt and brought healing to them both.

In 2012 while out shopping with a friend, we decided to visit the grave of her grandparents as we were driving near that area. Unknown to me my friend was concerned that while on a recent visit to the graveyard she had an uneasy feeling anytime she walked towards the back of the graveyard. She wanted to see if I thought anyone buried in that area needed assistance. Here she tells her story:

SORRY MA!

Monica

On a day's outing with Bríd I took the opportunity to ask her to visit the graveyard where my grandparents are buried. When we got there I did not mention to Bríd the reason I asked her to come with me was that I felt someone buried near the back of the graveyard may need assistance as I had been getting an uneasy feeling recently any time I walked past that area. While

I prayed at my family plot Brid did her own thing walking up and down the graveyard. When she came back she said all was well.

Then as we were leaving she said she would quickly check at the back of the graveyard as she had not gone all the way down. Brid was standing on the pathway beside a grave with the front of the headstone turned away from her so she had no way of knowing who was buried there. I joined her and stood at the other side of the grave. It was a local family plot and included a young man who had committed suicide. She sat on the kerb and started to do a crossing.

She told me his biggest regret was the pain he had caused his mother. He sent his love to his mother and to his little daughter. He was so very sorry. While doing the prayers with him Brid said his father had come to bring him home to the light. Brid was facing the back of the headstone and had no other way of knowing that his father had also been buried there and that the young man was survived by a daughter. I now know he is at rest.

WHO ARE YOU

I believe that before we are even born we decide, with the help of our guides, what lessons we want to learn from this life in order to progress our souls. For example we may choose to work on lessons around confidence, leadership, humility, abandonment issues, selflessness, or self-belief. We then are guided to choose where and to whom we will be born in order that we can best learn these life lessons.

If for example we have chosen to work on confidence and self-belief we may be born to a family where one parent is over-dominant, very controlling or even abusive. As we grow within this environment we can choose to become like the dominant parent or choose to be like the very quiet, sensitive and submissive parent in order to survive this period of our life.

The quiet, sensitive, submissive child can then be an easy target in school and continue the pattern on into adulthood and adult relationships, possibly dating or marrying a controlling partner until they finally learn to value themselves. The pattern established in their early life may be to stay quiet in the hope that the parent, teacher, school bully, employer, partner will stop shouting, stop being nasty and stop hurting them. They may finally come to understand that their needs are of equal importance. As they learn to value and respect themselves they learn that they do not always have to be the one to back down.

Hopefully the soul that has chosen this life lesson will at some point learn to say no. Sometimes the "NO", when it finally comes, can seem inappropriate to the situation. The straw that broke the camel's back may seem trivial to the other person and not warrant the force of the "NO" when it finally comes. The person having learnt to say "NO" may now take this new stance on everything. Having been the victim for so long they are now determined never to go back to that place of weakness. The challenge now is learning to balance how and when to say no and how to safely stand up for themselves and when to let it go or how to use their voice to find common ground.

Now if we flip the coin and look at the victim's sibling who chose to follow the controlling parent's example, their challenge is the opposite. They have chosen to act out the example of the over powering parent and grow up being the bully not allowing for any other point of view or anyone else's needs to be met outside of their own. But this sibling also has as much need for their soul to learn and grow. Instead of learning how to finally stand up for themselves and say no, their lesson is how to say yes and to actually hear other points of view and needs. They have to learn to look outside of themselves and to consider how their actions affect others.

As their victim sibling has always said yes, as have the other people they have gathered around them, they have never had to stop and consider how they are in fact continuing the cycle of pain. Their sibling has now found their voice and said "NO" and the controlling sibling is totally bewildered, trying to make sense of the new circumstances. Hopefully this can be their chance to start learning their life lesson. If, however, their sibling, child, employee, work colleague has not yet learnt to say "NO" their challenge is to be aware that we all deserve equal respect and to bring healthy balance into our lives and relationships.

Both, even though coming to the table from opposite ends of the spectrum, are coming with lifelong habits of response behaviour. Since childhood these have been their learnt survival techniques, be it the hiding in the corner or shouting back even louder than the original aggressor.

As adults our challenge is to look back at the decisions our inner child made in those early years in deciding which traits suited us best and kept us safe. Now it is time to honestly look at our current lives and see if this behaviour is still in our best interest. We can thank our inner child that with the information available to us at the young age of five and our perception of our world we worked out what would protect us. Now it may be time to reassess our world with our new adult perception and all the knowledge we now have and make some brave changes.

Some children often take on the fixer role, trying to hold everything together and feeling responsible for everyone. A client told me she got a weekend job from the age of twelve to save up for Santa presents for her siblings as otherwise there wouldn't be any. Thus she took on the responsibility of the parent. She then continued on through her adult life feeling responsible for her now adult siblings.

Other children can then take the opposite stance. If I cry loud enough or long enough someone else will fix it for me. Some never step up and take responsibility for themselves and then continue as adults to surround themselves with partners, friends, family members who they call on to "fix it". The challenge for both these personalities is to find the healthy balance.

There is so much for us to learn as we pass from our teenage years to adulthood, from being provided for to becoming the provider, from dependent to independent. This is a vital time as we learn to stand on our own two feet and subconsciously decide what inherited life belief systems we are going to live our lives by.

It was my pleasure to assist a young man as he set out on this life journey. I reassured him that even when he emigrated he would never be alone as his angels, guides and deceased loved ones would be by his side.

NEW BEGINNINGS

John Fogarty Jnr.

Just like every other young man in Ireland I am not prone to sharing my feelings or concerns at all. In fact I believed suppressing my problems and insecurities was the best option. When I first met Bríd I was at the peak of depression with long-term back problems and I was very indecisive about my future.

For some reason the calm and comfort she radiated just made me feel comfortable and allowed me to open up to her spiritually. She fast tracked my physical recovery from any injuries I had one hundred per cent through her healing ability. But for me that's not the really impressive thing.

During my healing sessions with her, I could envisage my dead relatives and loved ones there beside me! I felt they were

*helping me through Brid, even putting a message of love and
hope in my mind. I felt invigorated and when I explained why,
Brid knew what I was going to say. She felt their presence and
relayed to me advice and love they offered which guided me, a
young college student, to my dream career overseas!*

*I am very lucky to know her and feel like she is making my
life and that of those around me so much happier and brighter.
She has helped unlock the me I dreamt of becoming, if that
makes sense? Now, I am just a normal guy, who is very happy
and healthy and I've got an incredible confident outlook on
life. I owe that in no small part to this incredible person.*

Our life lessons determine a lot of our life experiences, as
does our environment. Our blood line also plays a role. We are
each made up of a unique DNA sum from our four grandparents.
They in turn are a unique DNA sum of their four grandparents
and so on. No one else will ever carry this combination. We are
unique. This same DNA connects us to those gone before us,
even if we have never met them. You may notice babies and
young children with the same facial expressions of grandparents.
My nephew, on learning Irish dancing, surprised his teacher by
dancing the old style steps even though he had never seen them
danced. She concluded the steps were in him!

Summertime 2013 I met an American tourist who felt
compelled to tell me his life story. His grandfather had married
a Native American. At the time of their marriage it was frowned
upon to marry someone from a different culture. The newly-
weds moved to a different state where they were not known and
it remained the family secret.

This tourist had only shared the knowledge of his ancestry with very few people, choosing not even to tell most of his friends or work colleagues. He in turn had married and had children. Their youngest child, a daughter, had been born with severe learning difficulties. Yet this child occasionally used Indian words. Recently when he had put her to bed she had spoken an Indian word while staring at the foot of her bed and smiling. What made this all the more strange was he knew this word was the name his Indian grandmother had been called by. He wondered if the child was in fact seeing his grandmother's spirit. If so, was she teaching the child their old language, or was the language just in her?

I believe our DNA does play a role in determining who we are, but it does not define us, no more than our life lessons. We choose the path we take. As we progress and release our limiting beliefs, these in turn will no longer need to be passed on to our children and grandchildren. Any negative karma that we have accumulated in this lifetime that we can now address and make restitution for will no longer need to be carried forward to future blood lines. We can make a difference as we strive for progression in a positive manner, not only for ourselves, but also for future generations and at the same time helping past generations to heal.

A friend sent me the following story about her little daughter, which is a perfect example of inherited intelligence that can't be explained logically.

GENIE MAC

Louise Carey

My granny died when I was twenty-one and she was the only grandparent in my life; the others died when I was young or before I was born. She was a fantastic lady, she worked from morning until night, but she was also great fun and had a way of understanding and way of talking to young people. She helped rear most of her grandchildren including me, so she was a huge influence in my life. Now that I am a mother of a little girl nearly three and a little boy fourteen months I talk to Granny a lot and ask for her help in different obstacles that come with being a mother.

A few months ago I was trying to get my little girl to sleep in a bed on her own. She was quite upset and just wouldn't settle so I asked Granny to please be with my little girl and rub her head and soothe her like she used to do for us. I felt an almost sudden sense of peace and calm come over me. I really felt her presence in the room and it gave me strength. My little girl did settle and it took a few nights like that of calling on Granny!

Then there are times when my little girl says something that reminds me of Granny and it makes me laugh. One day she was going around saying "genie mac" a lot. I couldn't think where she heard it. She couldn't tell me where she heard it because the last person I heard saying that was my granny. That was one of her little sayings and I took it as a sign to let me know that she is there watching over us.

Another day Isabelle, that is my little girl's name, was saying to me "your grandma's name is ???" But I couldn't understand her because it didn't sound like any of my grandmother names, but she kept saying it. Finally I made out that she was saying "your grandma's name is MOTHER" and she confirmed it when I said it. I thought: "My God, who is talking in your ear, little girl?!" That is what my granny's children, as in my dad and mom, (who was her daughter-in-law) and my aunty and uncles used to call her. Again since she died fourteen years ago I haven't heard it since then! My mom and dad got a great kick out of that one!"

AS WE SOW, SO SHALL WE REAP!

We are fortunate in that there are now so many self-help books, CDs and DVDs available to buy, borrow or get at the library. Often the difficulty is choosing which one to get. I personally like using affirmations. I have a calendar on my kitchen worktop with a daily affirmation so I get to start my day with a positive thought. They are short affirmations but they always make me smile and have the feel-good factor. My affirmation for today being "today I gladly get rid of all thoughts and beliefs I no longer need so that new ones can take their place. In the process, I bring much joy into my life".

In chapter 1 "A Sensitive Child" we looked at how energy can become blocked or negative emotions can linger in a building or on an item of jewellery or furniture. Similarly, we can have blocks in our own emotions or attitudes that we have carried with us since our early childhood. Once we have identified our personal blocks we can set about releasing them and moving forward.

I make up affirmations relevant to whatever is going on in my life at that time, or for whatever I want to draw into my life while releasing that which no longer serves me. I like to have my affirmations rhyme and be upbeat as they then make me feel good. By chanting or singing these affirmations we can bring even more positive energy to the situation. For example while walking when I come to a hill I chant:

"My body grows healthy fit and slim as I walk up and down this hill."

Because I like rhyming, my friends sometimes ask me to write rhymes relevant for them, so for a single girlfriend I suggested she chant:

"My perfect man is here at last

My disastrous dates are in the past

He is my soul mate, its plain to see,

And the girl he loves – wow that's me!"

While working on this book I have been saying my daily affirmation:

"My book is in print
the healing now sent.
The love that it holds
around the world unfolds.
On the bestselling list
it can't be missed.
Thank you Angels, Guides, Spirits
One and all
for pushing me to answer this call.
I am as happy as can be,
The truth within has set me free."

Affirmations can be used to address our more limiting beliefs:

I am a good person.

I believe in myself.

I let go of my need of criticism, criticism of self, criticism of others and criticism by others of me.

I now lovingly assert myself.

I am willing to release the pattern within me that is creating this condition/situation.

I move into the winning circle.

I love my job.

I am surrounded by people who care about me.

I release the past. I am flexible.

I love and approve of myself.

I love and approve of my body.

I choose to allow every adult to be responsible for themselves.

I am blessed beyond my fondest dreams.

I forgive myself.

I now have the strength and courage to deal with today and each new day.

I deserve the best and I accept the best now.

It is safe to trust life.

I am safe.

Choose whatever is relevant to your personal situation and repeat the statement as often as possible. Saying the statement while addressing yourself in a mirror can make the affirmation more real. However, you must at the same time pay attention to your thoughts. If you are confirming "all my needs are met" while sighing every time you get a bill, write a cheque, get your payslip, you are undoing all your good work.

Reading self-help books has really got me to look at my world and personal experiences in a different light. Am I the creator of the life experiences I have encountered? Am I responsible for the balance in my bank account? Has my inherited mantra "money does not grow on trees" got something to do with what I believe I am worth? What of my past and present relationships? Is the fact that I believed I should always put other people's needs before mine the reason why my past partners always put their needs before mine? Thank God for my wake-up call.

Over the past five years I have taken the time to look at my own various health conditions. In 2004 my husband and I sold our business in The Midlands and moved to my home place in the west of Ireland. The house we built was to be our family home, but in our hearts we both knew this was never going to happen. Our marriage was failing and so was my health.

I had reverted to my childhood method of dealing with pain by shutting down; if I couldn't feel the pain then it would not be able to hurt me. This is how I chose to deal with the pain of my marriage, built on broken dreams where I had lost the person I once was, I had given away my power and control in the vain hope that this would hold my marriage together. Now my body had taken my childhood coping mechanism to the extreme and developed a nerve disorder. I would frequently lose sensation in my limbs and occasionally I lost the entire use of my limbs. Thankfully it would usually only present on the right side, but not always. The simplest tasks became impossible. Some mornings I would be unable to raise my arm high enough to brush my hair or wash my teeth. I was unable to judge temperature with my limbs and had to use a thermometer when washing. I was sent for lots of tests and scans. Eventually, after ruling out some very scary illnesses, I was told that I could not break down vitamin B. This in turn had caused damage to the nerve endings in my body.

I took time to consider my health, my coping methods of shutting down and my belief that I must put others first. I recalled myself as the child getting repeatedly slapped by a nun that was teaching me at the age of six and how I had made the decision that if I could not feel the pain she could not hurt me. Now here I was again unable to feel pain. I burnt myself one day while I was preparing dinner; I looked at my blistered skin and thought that it must hurt so I had better put something on it!

In 2009 my marriage ended and my husband moved back to England. I had a lot of adjusting to do and a lot of issues I needed to address. I had pretended for many years to everyone including myself that everything was OK; now I needed to be honest, with myself at least. By making the decision not to feel pain I was sacrificing so many other aspects of my life, including my healing work.

I decided to trust myself to be my provider and for the first time in my life I learnt how to live on my own and take care of myself. I have finally come to a place where I am happy with who I am. I am now following my own path, not to please others but instead I am being true to myself. With this newly found strength and confidence my healing gift has also blossomed. The path I took to get here, often difficult and painful, has made me more empathic towards my clients and I feel better equipped by these experiences to work compassionately with those I meet.

One client who came to see me had been to various doctors, and had x-rays and scans done on the base of her spine. All had come back clear yet she constantly experienced pain in that area.

On asking her about her life she said, "Oh, you know, life is a pain in the ass." This was her mantra, the thought she repeatedly put out to the universe. The universe, having heard her request, provided her with exactly what she had been expecting: "a pain in the ass". She had become so used to saying, "life is a pain in the ass" that when I pointed this out to her she hadn't even been aware of what she was constantly saying. She decided to choose a new mantra!

A primary teacher came to see me. She was also experiencing back pain. She had been to various doctors and chiropractors and so on, and had x-rays and scans done. This time the pain was in her lower spine and down her legs. Again all the tests had come up blank. Yet this woman could hardly stand up straight. The spirits showed me that this was a person who really valued her friendships and was extremely loyal and trustworthy. When I repeated this back to her she agreed and said she never broke a secret. Anyone who had shared a problem with her she had kept their secret safe in her hip pocket.

I asked her to explain. She said that since she was a little girl she pictured herself putting her friends' secrets and problems in her hip pocket. This was her way of not breaking a confidence. She would visualise their secrets being put in her pocket where they would remain safely. We discussed this and I explained that carrying other people's burdens does not make them go away. The friends who had the problem in the first place, still had their various issues; they had not been diminished by the fact that she was holding on to a copy of their problem.

We will all be sympathetic to our friends' problems, but remember they are their problems. Only the adult with the problem has the power to solve or improve the situation. Carrying around a duplicate of someone else's problems, worrying about them, not sleeping and making ourselves ill will not improve the situation for our friend. Absolutely we should listen and we should care about their well-being. But do not make yourself sick carrying around a duplicate of someone else's issues.

I suggested she visit a church, light some candles and visualise herself emptying out her pocket with all her friends' secrets and problems and handing them back to God. Her body simply could not carry the weight of everyone's problems. It was also getting in the way of her personal journey and her life lessons.

There is a story about a man walking down the road when he comes to a large hole. When he peers in the hole he struggles to see the bottom as it is so deep and dark. After a while his eyesight adjusts to the darkness, he realises there is someone down in the depths of the darkness. At first he considers climbing down to the other person but then realises they would then both be trapped and unable to help each other. He decides that by staying out of the hole he will be of most use. He gets a long ladder and some more people to help and between them they are able to assist the person in need.

Sometimes when I meet clients who are very ill their partners or parents are struggling to accept and deal with the situation. If I were to start crying or getting emotionally attached to the gravity of their illness I would be of no use to anyone. Similarly if we get over-involved in someone else's problems, we are less likely to be of real assistance to them.

We each have our own journey. We need to deal with our own issues. I suggest that if you are worried about friends, family members, colleagues and others you can pray that they will find a solution and that God will help them to carry their burden.

It's great if we can help but we do not have to always come up with the solutions or the answers. If we are always providing the solution we can actually disempower our friends and they may never learn to come up with their own solutions and could come to depend on others to solve everything for them. They may never learn to take care of themselves and never learn their own life lessons.

There's a story of the traveller who comes to a new city and is greeted at the gate. The traveller asks: "What are the people like in your city?" The gatekeeper replies, "What are the people like in the city you left?" The traveller replies "The people there are all selfish and mean and are only interested in their own needs." And the gatekeeper responds "That is the kind of people you will find here as well." The traveller moved on.

Soon another traveller approaches the gatekeeper and asks him: "What are the people like in your city?" The gatekeeper replies to the second traveller: "Tell me about the people in the city that you have left." This traveller responds: "Well, the people are kind and giving and make the very best kind of friends." The gatekeeper gives the same response: "And those are the kind of people you will find in this city as well."

A lot of us suffer from the "far away hills are green" syndrome. The sibling who missed school days, got a low paying uninspiring part-time job and now lives with and cares for her ageing parents may resent the sibling who went to college, goes to her well-paid job with her expensive clothes in a fancy car and holidays with her perfect family. Whereas the sibling who put herself through college now sees herself as working around the clock trying to meet financial commitments and provide for her children's expectations and may resent the younger sibling who sailed through school without a care, sleeps in, hardly works and has no financial worries, as she will inherit the family home.

Rather than comparing our situation to that of others we need to learn to love ourselves, how we live our lives and how we spend our time. If we have made some bad choices it's time to make some good ones. Loving ourselves does not need to be expensive we can give ourselves time to go for a walk, put on a meditation CD when the kids are in bed, meet up with a friend, turn up the music in the kitchen while doing chores and sing, or take the floor brush for a dance around the kitchen, paint, play music, gardening, whatever it is that makes our soul sing. It is time to love ourselves or at least start the process of learning how to love ourselves.

Think big thoughts, but relish small pleasures. As we start to believe we are worth the time and effort, positive changes will begin to come into our lives. We will be better equipped to deal with the negativity in our lives. We can then swap our "far away hills are green" for "there's no place like home" and learn to appreciate the here and now.

From time to time I have siblings book in to see me. It used to amaze me how different their issues were. Despite being brought up in the same home with family members who have shared the same occasions, celebrations and difficulties, they are very different individuals.

We all have a unique perception of events. Anyone working in law enforcement or with an interest in detective/crime viewing will notice that, irrespective of how many eye witnesses there are to an event, they all give a different account of what happened. We each come to the event with our own issues and outlook on life, whether we are the victim, the aggressor, or the survivor. We all have our own unique strands of DNA and our own life lessons. We each carry our own baggage and we each have a different perspective of an event. It is this unique perception and its impact on our life that we carry forward to the next event, and so on.

The house I grew up in was a typical country cottage. It is approximately one hundred and fifty years old, with huge internal walls, old open fireplaces and high ceilings. It felt safe and we were loved. The children kept arriving until there were finally eight kids. This was an era of extended families and so my grand-aunt and her husband also lived with us. My maternal grandfather lived out his final years with us and at another stage my uncle lived with us when his health deteriorated. Eventually the time came to build an extension. This replaced the old lean-to kitchen and gave us a bathroom for the first time and a large new bedroom. It had a flat roof extension which joined the old building.

When I was about eight I was sleeping in the new extension, my baby brother was asleep in his cot, and on the other side of him my two-year-old brother was sleeping in his little bed. The kitchen had an old solid fuel range and above this was a clothes line, where our school uniforms were drying after walking home in the rain the kilometre from the school bus stop. My father kept and killed his own pigs and there would always be large pieces of smoked bacon hanging over the range. On this occasion my parents, grand-aunt and three older siblings were in the old part of the house. They had watched the news and said the rosary.

Unknown to them a hole had formed in an old saucepan that my mum had been simmering on the range. Its contents poured across the top of the range; this in turn caused the bacon fat to start melting and dripping onto the range. That entire part of the house completely filled with thick black smoke. The only memory I have is waking up outside the house with my brother gripping me by the neck and shoulders and shouting at me. He was crying and trying to wake me up. At first I thought someone was trying to strangle me as I had inhaled so much smoke and could not breathe. (Up until recently if anyone touched my neck or shoulders I would respond as if fighting for my life.)

As the eight-year-old girl trying to understand the events I just wanted my parents but I could not see them and then realised they were taking care of my two youngest siblings. This added to my established perception that my parents appeared to care more about my younger siblings than they did about me.

Some months ago I was having tea with my brother, my hero, and we got chatting about the events of that night. He had only been ten at the time but clearly remembered every detail. After the rosary had finished he had gone to the kitchen to make tea. He went to turn on the light as it was so dark, then realised the light was already on and the reason he could not see was because the room was full of smoke. He realised what was happening.

He said his only thought at the time was that I was in the bedroom. I was nearest to him in age and we always played together, he said to be honest at the time he hadn't considered the two younger children. Without any thoughts for his own safety he had gone to the bedroom and somehow found my bed in the thick blackness of smoke. Despite the fact he was now struggling to breathe he had lifted me out unconscious and carried me past my parents to safety. It was only at this stage that my parents realised what was happening and gone to save the younger children who were still lying unconscious in the smoke-filled bedroom.

For some thirty years I had secretly held feelings of hurt and disappointment that I had meant less to my parents than my younger siblings. Whereas in fact all this time, I had been the first child to be rescued that night. Being eight I hadn't appreciated that a baby and a two-year-old need so much attention, which I undoubtedly had received when I was their age. I had lived out the remainder of my childhood and adulthood with my perception of events that night. Our perception of events goes a long way in creating who we are and the person we become.

The following testimonial tells the story of a young man whose actions in haste led him to flee his homeland. His perception of what the consequences would be prevented his soul finding peace.

THE LANDLORD'S HAY

Mary Fogarty

I was first introduced to Bríd a couple of years ago. I had a few healing sessions with her and found this to be very beneficial for a number of minor ailments and gave me great consolation when my father died.

One day, out of the blue, my Aunt Breda said to me: "I met Pat K on the bus today going to the Day Care Centre and he said to me "You had a Grand-uncle Jim who had to flee to Australia in the troubled times because he got into trouble with the Brits." I had often heard my father talk of his Uncle Jim who indeed had to flee because he fell foul of the Authorities. Aunt Breda said: "Isn't it strange that he should say that now – maybe Jim needs a prayer." "And from that day onwards we both said a prayer for Jim every day.

Two years later I was having a healing session with Bríd. When it was over Bríd said to me: "Mary, a Jim came during the healing and I could see that he was troubled about something that happened in his youth." Bríd could see a troubled family and a reek of hay on fire. She then described a young man walking away from the family cottage leaving his parents and younger siblings behind. There was a sense of injustice and a terrible sadness. She was then shown Northern Australia." I got such a jolt as the only Jim I had ever heard of in the family was indeed the grand-uncle referred to by my Aunt Breda.

I told Bríd the story and she could see the entire event. I discussed the story with my brother who, unknown to me, had known the full story from my father.

What had happened was that during the troubles it transpired that Jim's family had purchased hay from a local landlord, through the landlord's agent and because there was no room for it in their hay barn it was stored by the said landlord on his farm. Winter came, and as it transpired, it was a particularly cold and harsh winter and fodder was in very short supply nationwide. Because of this shortage the landlord decided to misappropriate the hay and give it to one of his absentee landlord friends. The landlord's agent came to Jim's parents, informed them of what was intended and returned the purchase money to them. This, of course, put Jim's family's animals in danger of starvation because there was nowhere else to get fodder. When Jim learnt what had happened he went to the landlord's agent, gave back the money and set fire to the hay. He realised the following morning that he would have to flee the country immediately. He left straight away for Australia and no contact was received from him after that.

Bríd said that when she visualised the event during the healing session with me she could see a whole family's upset. She said that Jim, with no way of contacting his family in Ireland, always worried that his actions had created difficulties for his family with the ruling British authorities after his departure. He needed to release the cords that held him which would enable him to cross over to the light. She did the crossing there and then with me. It was a beautiful ceremony and I felt privileged to be part of it.

Some weeks later Bríd did a further healing with me and when it was over she said: "Jim was here and he said to say: "Thank you, we are all happily reunited now."

I was totally fascinated by the sequence of events and how Jim's message came to us in such a roundabout way in the first instance and then to come through Bríd during the healing session.

As a footnote I have since learnt that the landlord in question and my family became very friendly and realised that a great injustice had been done at the time.

HEALING HANDS

Over the years my client list has steadily grown and I have met so many amazing people when I get to share some of their deepest most personal moments. Sometimes I am shown glimpses of deeply personal and traumatic events without realising their significance. When the healing finishes I quickly do a re-cap in my own mind of what I have been shown, and frequently I question my ability, thinking the client will be disappointed with how little I have been shown. But I know by now not to question the fact that spirit knows best and that whatever healing and spiritual evidence is appropriate will always come through. The night Eimear came for healing I was thinking to myself that she would be disappointed as the only evidence I had for her was of her mum busy reading and Bluee the cow. I hadn't appreciated that what I was shown was a reference to the singly most traumatic event in her entire childhood.

I always take the time to reassure my clients that the healing process is never scary. They will receive whatever healing or evidence they are meant to. They may feel heat to areas in their body or they may see colours or feel a tingling sensation; others may experience scent memories. No two sessions are ever the same. The level of the healing received is always in line with the person's own spiritual development. It is never frightening, it is sent from a space of pure love.

Sometimes, however, I forget to reassure myself. I can let my logical brain take over and end up in a state of nerves wondering if the client will be disappointed with what I pick up on. "What if I don't get any evidence to share? What if, after travelling for hours they get nothing? What if someone locally comes to see me and gets nothing? What if I lose my reputation?" I have frequently gotten myself in a complete state, but then remind myself that I am not the one doing the healing. I remind myself to put my ego aside, as by panicking I am not questioning my ability but that of the Divine, my guides, the angels and those in spirit world who come forward to connect with the client. I apologise, make tea, calm down and get ready to welcome the client.

My guides and angels have worked incredibly hard over the years to help train me in the use of my gift. When I finally made the decision to share this gift with the general public I was amazed with the synchronicity of those who made appointments. During the first six weeks of doing healing in The Midlands a large percentage of my clients all presented with breathing problems.

When I started the healing session for one of my first clients, I was shown a picture of the human anatomy in my mind's eye, as if a biology book was being held up in front of me. The picture then focused on the lungs. It was some fifteen years since I had studied biology and I had forgotten most of it. I was shown what looked like bunches of grapes and remembered these are called the alveoli. But in this circumstance these were not filling as they should be. In my own body I could feel a sensation behind the top of my nose as if there was a small blockage there, I also felt light-headed. Putting the picture and the clairsentient feelings together I was able to tell the client that there seemed to be a small blockage in his nasal passage which in turn meant there was not always sufficient oxygen making its way to his lungs. This would put his system under pressure when doing strenuous exercise, even running up stairs, and may cause him to occasionally feel light-headed. I explained that healing was being sent to this area and that he could follow up with a doctor and/or add breathing exercises to his daily routine. His healing session then went on to include spirit evidence.

The next client was a teenage boy. Again I had no idea of any physical condition he had. The picture of the anatomy reappeared in my mind's eye, this time concentrating on the trachea/windpipe. Two days later I had a female client where I was shown a shadow on the lower left lung. After my training in the breathing system was completed a large percentage of the next group of clients (travelling from various parts of the country) presented with backache, muscular pains and poor posture. Once I had mastered an understanding of these conditions the next group again had similar physical issues. Now I can pick up much quicker what my guide is showing me; a quick reference to that issue is sufficient. This then allows my guide to put more time and effort into training me on a new aspect of healing. And so my training continues.

The majority of my clients ask to see me in relation to a physical ailment but then the session can take numerous turns and we end up discussing a difficult childhood memory, or an inability to speak up for fear of reprisal, a fear of relationships, financial pressures, abuse, depression, and so on. No two healing sessions are ever the same. Occasionally the sole purpose of the client visit is simply physical healing as was the case for the next testimonial.

SURVIVAL KIT

Delphia

On a cold wet evening in Dublin I was out with some friends of mine when I slipped on a wet surface and fell flat on my back. After a long ordeal in the emergency room I was seen by the staff. The x-rays showed I had broken the back bone of my left leg (the tibia) and also the space between my ankle and leg bones had considerably widened. A few days later after a lot of swelling had finally gone down, I had surgery.

I was put under general anaesthetic to have a plate and screws put into my leg to piece it back together. The doctor affirmed my operation had gone well but that I had also torn some ligaments on the same leg. It would be a long road to recovery. They prescribed a list of drugs and painkillers to take for the next month or up until my next appointment in four weeks' time. A few days later I was sent home, with a cast on my leg, for nine weeks of non-weight bearing. I had a list of tablets to take and I knew when the next ones were to be taken as I could feel a pulsating pain in my leg.

The cocktails of tablets were now my survival kit. Sleeping in the same position for days definitely became a challenge.

Using crutches were sore on my hands; even going to the toilet was an ordeal. I thought over in my mind how simple things can change our life in a matter of seconds. I was now out of work for weeks and then I would have to work from home for the next few months as I could not get up the stairs in the office building. And I was then told that there were months of physio to look forward to. It was a trying time but I knew I had to look forward and not back and so I did.

I was delighted to hear the news Bríd was paying me a visit. She arrived three days after the operation.

This was definitely a time when I suddenly knew who my real friends were and the appreciation I had for my family as they sacrificed time to help me and put a smile on my face. It was hugely appreciated. Bríd always puts a smile on my face and I was really looking forward to her arrival. As always the first point of action was to put the kettle on.

My body, however, was under a lot of pressure because of the cocktail of drugs I was feeding it. All of them prescribed. My stomach was certainly feeling worse for wear. I spoke with Bríd and she then began her healing.

When she heals her hands hover over my body. Even with my eyes closed I know where her hands are above my body because of the heat that radiates from them. She got to my broken leg and when her hands came to the point where I had the operation, I felt like the muscles were being gently rolled and massaged underneath the skin layer. Keeping in mind my leg is in a cast. It is actually a very hard sensation to try and explain but I knew it was only doing good so I took a breath and let the healing in.

Like any spiritual healing I have ever had with Bríd I always feel great afterwards, like weights have been lifted from around me. I settled in that night expecting the usual uneasiness and the need to consult my survival medical kit every few hours. I must have fallen asleep around midnight as I remember watching TV but the next thing I knew I had woken and turned to take my tablets when I noticed the clock saying nine thirty a.m. I could not believe it. How did I not wake up in pain before this time? Next thing my brain recognised was my leg and a sick feeling entered my stomach expecting a horrible pain about to register with me as I had neglected to take the drugs during the night. But I really felt no pain or any unusual sensations or even any sign of sleeping uncomfortably during the night. Where was I? What had happened? I was so confused. I decided not to take any tablets to see when the pain would actually kick in again. It never did.

From that morning onwards, four days after the operation and the morning after receiving healing from Bríd I did not take any more painkillers. I called the hospital and asked them how long they thought I would need to take the tablets they had prescribed to me. The reply was a shocking four more weeks. I was healed from pain in a matter of hours. By late that evening my body had totally relaxed and my stomach was back in action and I managed to eat something. I couldn't believe it. I mean I could, it was just hard to. I called Bríd immediately with the awesome update.

Miraculously, Bríd had the survival healing kit I needed all along I just didn't realise it at the time. Thank you Bríd and thank God for healing my unbearable pain and giving me peace of mind and body again.

Babies and young children are generally much more open and accepting of channelled healing than teenagers or adults. As we grow we tend to accept everything that adults tell us, we build protective barriers around ourselves with our newly acquired belief systems, our perceptions and life experiences. When I am asked to channel healing for babies or young children it is much easier for me to connect with their true essence as they do not have "walls" up. Their subconscious mind is not questioning the healing that is being sent; they just accept it. Whereas with adults I really have to explain the process and make the client feel safe enough to let down their barriers before they will accept any healing.

I am most comfortable doing healing in person, ideally in my own treatment room where I can fully relax during the process. However, this is not always possible and so occasionally I will agree to channel distance healing for which I need a photo of the client and I need to be able to see the face clearly and ideally the eyes open so that I can connect with the person in need. The following story submitted by Laura, the mother of a little boy whom I had never met but as he was so open to receiving healing the process proved very successful for him.

CONOR

Laura Carey

My little boy Conor became violently sick last year just before his first birthday. He was listless, had an exceptionally high temperature and had explosive diarrhoea (every twenty minutes – penetrating nappies and clothes) and vomiting. This was his first time since birth being sick.

My GP (also a paediatrician) diagnosed E. coli 125. This is the third most dangerous form of E. Coli in young children. My GP told me that there was no treatment available; only to keep him isolated and hydrated. He also told us to watch him vigilantly as it could deteriorate very quickly and cause renal failure. He also informed us that it could take weeks for it to clear out of Conor's system.

Conor's condition began to worsen and my husband's aunt passed on Brid's number (whom I'd never met) and asked me to forward a photo of Conor with his eyes visible and a note saying that my little boy was very sick. I did as asked.

That day I received a phone call from Brid telling me that Conor had E. Coli and that he would start to feel much better soon. She also mentioned my mum was watching over him (she passed away eleven years ago).

Within an hour of Brid's phone call, Conor's appetite returned completely to normal (after a week of only fluids), playing normally (after lying listlessly for a week, totally non-responsive) and his happy, bubbly temperament had returned to normal.

This was such a surreal recovery and so effective. I was amazed that Brid could tell me what was wrong with my little boy just by looking at a photo. Brid also told me how he had contracted the illness from a stray black labrador (that we had encountered at an outdoor restaurant the previous Sunday).

I was absolutely blown away by Brid and her amazing sense of spirituality. It gave me great peace of mind to know my mum was watching over my little boy. I will be eternally grateful to Brid for helping Conor recover so rapidly. You are an amazing woman, Brid. Love and gratitude.

To be in the company of the client is definitely the strongest connection for me. Failing this I can make a connection if I have a recent photo and always I need the permission of the client. However, when chatting with close friends and family by phone, because I know them so well and know they are open to receiving channelled healing, without even trying, I will occasionally become aware of any physical problems they are experiencing. Spirit world is very careful to only show me physical weaknesses on these occasions as it would not be appropriate for me to be shown emotional issues or past experiences without the other person's expressed wishes. Because I have such a close relationship with my sister who now lives in Australia I knew when she had gone into labour as I could feel her contractions.

Occasionally the person who phones me for help is not the person who is ill, yet I am still able to make the connection. This is because the person I am speaking with is thinking about the sick person while speaking with me, as was the case in the next testimonial.

WORD OF MOUTH

John Francis

One day I was speaking to a friend who said he had a lingering throat problem and because of his failure to shake it off, he was becoming more and more concerned about it. I told him about our family friend, Bríd, who was a spiritual healer and he said he would be very open to receiving healing from her. I promised him I would contact her later that evening when she returned from work.

Later that afternoon I met another neighbour and we spoke at length about the fact that he had been diagnosed with cancer of the throat. He was receiving treatment and was naturally worried about the cancer spreading.

As promised I rang Bríd and told her I had a friend with a throat problem and would like to arrange an appointment for him. Without hesitation she replied that the cancer had not reached the lymph glands and would not spread. Instantly I realised that over the phone she was picking up, from me, the symptoms of the second neighbour to whom I had spoken shortly before I rang her.

The outcome of this particular incident was that I related the full story to both men, they both attended Bríd for healing and both recovered fully. They remain in good health at the time of writing almost five years later. That was the first instance that I was aware of Bríd's ability of picking up on a person's symptoms over the phone.

We later discovered that sending her a photo of the patient made it possible for her to diagnose and send healing. This indicated a strengthening and further development of her great gift. Not only had she the gift of diagnosis, feeling the pain and location of your ailment in her own body, she also had the gift of calling forth and transferring healing to the location in your body where it was required.

EGGS AND HEARTACHE

A reoccurring issue that comes up time and again for clients is broken hearts. Frequently during healing sessions I see streams of green light coming in to help heal old hurts. Recently while doing healing with a teenager I was shown a picture of a heart as if drawn by a young child with a bandaid on it. I then saw in my mind's eye the client as a very young child, just about old enough to walk. She was sitting on the floor in a sitting room. The child was crying and looked so sad. I asked the teenager if she remembered what had happened. She had no memory of the event but knew that she was about eighteen months old when her father had walked out. She said she had no memory of her father and did not feel any loss from his departure. Yet her inner child had been affected and had, even at that young age, noticed the change in her environment.

Often clients are in troubled relationships or have just finished a relationship and wonder where they can now find new love. Similar to our "far away hills are green" syndrome I explain that first we have to learn to love ourselves before we draw someone else in. Like attracts like. If we are coming from a difficult relationship we may be feeling broken, with low self-esteem and low motivation. As the law of attraction states, like attracts like, so chances are we will be drawn to people who are at the same level as us. Someone who is very content, settled, motivated with high self-esteem, may feel pity for us, but they are unlikely to be drawn to start a relationship with someone with very low confidence. First we should work on repairing ourselves. It is important that we learn how to love ourselves before contemplating another relationship or we may find ourselves in another unhealthy relationship.

After my marriage ended I thought for a while that the world had also ended. I was afraid of living a life on my own. I believed that I needed someone else (anyone else) to help with the daily tasks of running a home. I worried about financial aspects of day-to-day living. I missed the companionship of having someone to talk to.

Thankfully my cousin was visiting from America at the time. He sat me down for a long chat. He explained the importance of learning to care for myself. First I had to learn that I didn't need someone else to take care of me, that I could take care of myself. Only then would I be in a position to love someone just for that reason. I wouldn't be choosing to be with them out of need but rather I would be with them because I enjoyed their company and wanted to be with them.

As part of his explanation he drew eggs. Since then I have used his diagram with many of my clients. I ask my clients to picture themselves as an egg and to draw a line across it. Above the line represents the issues or baggage we are carrying at this time. Below the line represents our current level of self-esteem. Our aim is to move the line north as much as possible. The further up the egg we can progress before starting a new relationship, the healthier it will be and the better chance it has of working out.

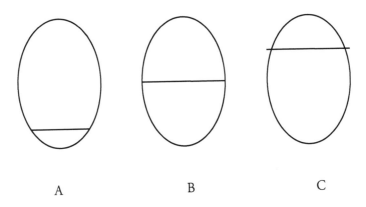

Time and events can also change us and our needs. Your current relationship may have started out with two eggs from the A basket but now that you have been working on your affirmations and self-worth you find you have moved to basket B and find your partner still in with the A team. So what now? Is it time to make an omelette? Your partner may be inspired by the new you and follow your example. Or you may be able to continue working on your self-worth in your aim to join the C team and be unaffected by your partner's fears or lack of insight to progress with you. If not, then you need to decide whether you can still find happiness in this relationship.

ROSES

William T

The first time I had the opportunity to get some healing, I didn't have a clue what it was all about! My siblings and family were getting some healing done by Bríd at our family home. I didn't really know Bríd at the time but she offered me some healing. I was intrigued and open to the idea, so I was grateful and said I'd give it a go.

I sat down amongst the crew at the kitchen table and Bríd stood beside me and put her hand over my head. So I closed my eyes and sat back and relaxed. Although my eyes were closed I could see a lot of green and yellow, like you would if you were dreaming. I felt very relaxed and my stomach started to grumble a bit. Although I couldn't see or feel Bríd's hands, I thought they were moving all the time, really quickly, going up and down, around my head, but when I asked the onlookers afterwards, they said that was not the case; her hands were still all the time.

The healing lasted for about ten minutes and I felt good after. I didn't say anything at first; Brid gave me some water and started to talk. She said there was a lot of green and yellow energy coming to me during the session. I was amazed she knew that, as I had seen those colours also. She said yellow was for my stomach which she felt needed a lot of healing. This was very true, as I had suffered from stomach ulcers for years.

She said the green was for my heart; emotionally, I was sad over a recent break-up and had locked it up rather than dealing with it. Brid said that while I talked to people about it when it happened, I hadn't admitted to myself that I was sad and as a result I had not gotten over it. I needed to acknowledge it to myself in order to heal. She said I didn't have to be a macho man all the time; I could acknowledge my feelings and work on them. When she explained this to me, I instantly knew she was right. When I admitted it to myself and spoke about it some more, I got over it pretty quickly and as a result I cheered up great. I hadn't realised that it was making me sad.

Brid said that some of my deceased relatives had come to help me during the healing and it was like they were queuing up during the session to come and help straighten my back and improve my posture. She said it was like they had their hands on my shoulders and their knees on my back, clicking my vertebrae back into place. She said this was something I needed to work on. She said my grand-aunt who had passed away around that time came to me briefly during the healing session and gave me a big hug. I was really amazed and could totally picture her doing that. She was a woman of few words and that would have been her style.

It was great to feel better after the session and also to have lots of things like my posture to work on for continued improvements. All that happened in the space of ten minutes. It was an amazing experience.

The second time I had healing, Brid gave me a ten minute session while I was hung-over. Poor Brid could feel the hangover during the healing. During the session I really felt the energy in my stomach. After the session Brid told me that my grand-uncle had come to me and given me a gift of a rose to *help me with romance. This was at a time when I was just ready to move on from my last experience, so it was great to know I had progressed from the last session!*

She said that my other late uncle also came to her during the healing. He showed her a scene from my childhood where he was swinging me in the air telling me I was a good boy. She described the scene, what I looked like and what I was wearing. Later that day I got out my baby photos and looked through them. I found a picture of that moment; it was unreal; she had even described the haircut and jacket I had at the time!

Bríd said I needed to work on my diet to help heal my stomach. She said that my legs were all strained as my shoes were too flat and had no arch supports. She felt that I would finish up on crutches as an old man if I didn't try correcting my posture. I was amazed at this as it was very true once I became conscious of it; I had never really paid attention to it.

After the session I went to a dietician who helped me identify food that aggravated my stomach. After a few weeks I really started to see an improvement. Bríd had healed my stomach and now that I had adjusted my diet I was no longer aggravating it. Happy days!

So then I went to a physio to get a sports massage on my legs. She said my legs were very bad; all my muscles were strained and they were rock hard. It took three deep tissue massage sessions to work out all the knots in the muscles. It was painful but I knew I had to do it. The physio sent me to get orthotics made: insoles tailor-made for my flat shoes; they corrected my walk and supported my feet. The physio also gave me exercises to stretch my leg muscles. Between the healing, the exercises, the massages and the orthotics my legs have really improved and continue to do so.

When I was growing up I was always my granny's pet at home! We were best friends all my life; she died around fourteen years ago. She came to me during the session and Bríd said that Granny wanted me to know she still thinks I'm the bee's knees! It was a lovely message to get.

I got healing one other time; I was really sick as I had picked up a violent vomiting bug. The timing was awful as I had tickets for one of my favourite bands the next night. The reunion tour of the Stone Roses, a band that I thought I would never get to see. It looked like there was no chance of me being well enough to go to it as it was on the next day.

Let me set the scene. The bug kicked off around six p.m. and I had been sick about three times and was still feeling really nauseous. It was like all the liquid in my stomach had turned really acidic. I tried taking Motillium and Rennie but they would not stay down and had zero effect.

Luckily my mom was talking to Bríd and told her I was sick. Bríd texted to say she would give me remote healing. I hated to be bothering her as it was around eleven p.m. at this stage but I was delighted she would help. So I took a picture of myself and I sent it to Bríd via text. I was in a bad way and although we were on opposite coasts of Ireland, I could feel the healing the second it started. It lasted for around twenty minutes.

I sat back on the couch and I closed my eyes. I could feel a lot of energy on my stomach during the session. I also saw a polar bear in my mind's eye as if I was dreaming. This was similar to the first session where I had seen green and yellow. Bríd has a great gift. I started to feel less nauseous right away, and she called me shortly afterwards. Bríd said I was very open to the healing. She could feel it going to me really strong as soon as she started. She said she could feel my sick stomach and said she thought it felt like bad food poisoning. She told me I was dehydrated and needed to drink 7Up, as it would rehydrate me and replace sugars in my system.

Bríd also mentioned that there was another poison in my body from a jellyfish sting I received a few weeks earlier on holidays. She said I needed lots of water and rest to flush it out of my system and let my body recover. Great advice. She wished me a speedy recovery and we said goodbye.

A few minutes later I remembered the polar bear and was disappointed I forgot to ask Bríd about it. Then my phone rang; for real, she said she meant to say that my granddads had come to visit during the healing; they wanted to let me know they were there for me. So I told her about the polar bear. She said that the polar bear was a message from my granddads; the bear is a strong animal but if it wants to get the honey it must leave its cave.

I was working from home a lot at the time. I was at home ninety per cent of the time and working on nixers after work until eleven p.m. most nights. So I knew myself that I needed to get out more. The message was to get outdoors in nature and get out more socially. So I took the advice on board, it was great to receive such relevant advice from my granddads, one of whom I had never met but I feel quite close to. Shortly after the call I got sick once more around one a.m. and astonishingly I *felt perfect after that. It was like my body got rid of all the effects of the bug from of my system. It was unreal. I was astonished I could feel so well so quickly after the condition I was in when I first spoke with Bríd.*

The next morning I was surprised how well I felt considering what had happened. I was well enough to go to work and even got to go to the gig that night. As far as I was concerned it really was a miracle. I was so happy Bríd had helped me out once again. I don't know where I would be without her.

I'm looking forward to the next time our paths cross. I'm not religious but Bríd helped me to realise that there is a spiritual world out there. I find it fascinating. It's great to think that our loved ones are out there and that they want to help and guide us on our way. Its great that people like Bríd exist who have the ability to make the connection and allow them to communicate with us. I'd really like to have her gift; I would ask them lots of questions and try to find out the meaning of life, what their lives are like now and how they spend their time.

THE FAMILY TREE

In 2009 a woman from Limerick, named Maureen, came to see me. She made the booking to get help with a physical condition but we ended up doing a lot of emotional healing. She had been having ongoing conflict with her family. Also, she explained her marriage was turbulent at best and abusive at its worst. Recently she had started standing up for herself. A heated disagreement, between her and her husband, escalated to other family members getting involved and taking sides. Her home life had become so difficult that she had moved out of the family house and was now staying with friends.

Throughout the healing I could see green light surrounding her, a sign of emotional healing being sent to her heart. We discussed forgiveness, which to me means a conscious decision to no longer hold the pain from the hurtful event. It does not mean the act did not take place or is justified; it just means that a decision is made to no longer give it power, time or thought. Normally when spirit world are showing me evidence of past or present events the pictures come and go very quickly. This was different. Every detail was shown to me in slow motion waiting while I relayed the information. I had never had evidence shown to me in such a detailed manner before. Her guide and those in the spirit world worked incredibly hard as this would have involved an exceptional amount of energy.

Maureen recognised all the spirits I described, except one. I described a woman in her thirties wearing a lovely knee-length summer dress that was clinched at the waist and then puffed out. It was white with red flowers stitched throughout. She was also wearing glasses that came to a point – typical of the fashion in the sixties. Maureen said she would have to do some research.

We also talked about God and spirituality in general. Because her home life had been so difficult Maureen had found herself questioning the existence of "a something else". At the end of the session, through the tears, Maureen told me she found the session very comforting, emotional and reassuring. Three days later she phoned me to say she had visited her mum specifically to find out about the mystery woman. It turned out to be her mother's sister who had died in her early thirties. Her mother took down an old photo to show her and it was exactly as per the evidence with her aunt wearing the dress and glasses. Maureen said they had spent a lovely evening together reminiscing about olden times. Two days later Maureen was killed in a car accident.

In the summer of 2010 I got a call from friends asking if I could see an acquaintance of theirs who was holidaying in Ireland and was feeling unwell. As I was free that evening I agreed to meet with them and they made their way to my home. Here John Francis recalls their visit and the events which followed:

SIBLINGS

John Francis

A friend of mine, his wife and some of their friends came to visit from France in the summer of 2010. He was a man of rare good humour and great wit and was much loved by all of us. We all went on a shopping trip to Galway.

All day he had complained of feeling under the weather and seemed to have a touch of flu or a virus. He mentioned three or four times that he believed he was dying. We paid little heed to his references to impending death, as he was a renowned joker and seemed to be really enjoying the day.

We had great fun, but at regular intervals he repeated that he believed he was close to death. Towards evening I told him about our friend, a spiritual healer, and suggested that we visit her. To my surprise (he had never previously showed any interest in religious or spiritual matters) he agreed instantly and so we rang Bríd to arrange an appointment. She agreed to see him that evening and we journeyed directly to her home.

The healing session with Bríd revealed viral symptoms and a couple of historic ailments. However, what most excited and fascinated my friend was that Bríd indicated that he had a brother and a sister, communicating with him from the spiritual world.

She said they had both died at birth but he had not previously been aware of their existence. They communicated incidents from his childhood of which only he was aware.

On our journey home from Bríd's house that night he did recall from his early memories his mother going to hospital to have a baby and returning home without one. There was no doubt now in his mind that he had a brother and sister in the spiritual world. On the journey home he talked about nothing only his newly discovered siblings and was already making plans to erect memorials for them. He returned to France the following day, still feeling under the weather.

A couple of days later he was involved in a car accident. He was admitted to hospital but did not appear to have any serious injury. Two days later, he died.

I do know that Bríd brought him great joy on that particular visit and we are all very grateful to her."

During his healing session all the evidence was shown to me in slow motion similar to what had happened during Maureen's session. Another similarity was that, prior to their healing sessions, both had questioned the existence of a higher power. The third similarity was the very strong and detailed evidence given, including that of deceased family members whose existence they were not previously aware of. The most shocking similarity for me was their imminent death. In trying to comprehend these experiences I wondered if the spirit world had worked extra hard in order to ensure both would recognise those spirits who came to meet them, at their time of death.

CROSSINGS

What I am asked the most questions about is the process I call crossings. To me it now all seems so ordinary that I often forget that what I am seeing and feeling is to the majority of people extraordinary. When spirits shows me their present reality it is set in the time frame of when they died. This can still take time for me to adjust to.

When travelling in Normandy, France, while visiting the grave of a client's grand-uncle as told in the story "Far away in Australia" we took a break at a travel stop. When I walked into the ladies' washroom I noticed the sinks and mirrors to my left and cubicles to my right. Then everything changed. I was now standing in the middle of a field with a peasant couple standing in front of me. The woman was a lot shorter than her husband; she was wearing a light brown jacket and skirt with a white lace frill fringe at the bottom of the skirt, and had on a neck scarf with a pretty pattern of little red flowers. Her husband had also dressed up for the occasion, and was wearing a light brown suit. They had come from the spirit world in search of their son, a young Hungarian man who had been conscripted into the army and had died in that field which is now a petrol stop. They had taken the opportunity of my visiting the location to get help for their child. At the time of his death he felt unable to cross to the light as he was appalled by the fact he had killed people who were not his enemies but had done so in order to save his own life.

I talked with the young soldier and explained I believe that God loves him as do his parents who were waiting to bring him home. Since his death he had continued living in the reality of the battlefield and was unable to see present day life or see those already passed on to the next world. As he listened to my words the haze lifted from around him and he could see his parents and was overjoyed to be reunited with them. I could feel an overwhelming sense of peace and love and he passed to the light. I was suddenly standing in the middle of the ladies' washroom. I have no way of knowing how long the experience lasted or what the other women in the washroom must have thought as they had to walk around me while I stood there in an apparent trance.

A lot of the crossings I have done had been while visiting graveyards. When I am assisting a trapped spirit the strongest connection with them for me will be if I am at the place where they died. This is not always possible. Because they have a connection to their grave I can tune into their spirit's essence while standing by their grave. Likewise if a family member of the deceased visits me and brings a photo of their relative I will be able to use the photo to make the connection. This is similar to doing healing for the living, where my strongest connection will be in person; failing this I will try to make a connection through a recent photograph.

I occasionally invite friends and students to accompany me when I know such an event is likely to take place. This helps them to more fully understand the process. Though it doesn't always go quite to plan! This proved to be the case in the following testimonial sent in by Delphia when we met the soul of a young boy called Thomas.

THOMAS

Delphia

Ahh, a weekend at Brid's – it's always going to be eventful!

Yes, I got the call earlier that week that Brid was going to be doing some crossings and the location was going to be a famine house located between Lahinch and Ennistymon. I felt great to be asked by Brid to assist her at the task at hand even though I didn't know how I would actually be assisting!

Nonetheless, I pottered down to Clare to hopefully witness some crossings. It began with a drive to the famine house and as we drew near Brid felt a very strong energy as though the spirits knew she was coming that day.

Then again if I was in spirit and could not cross over to continue my journey I would be waiting too. A monument that had been erected in the memory of all the souls who left their earthly bodies during the famine period had become the chosen spot. Anyone reading or hearing about crossings for the first time might believe it to be a spooky experience being carried out in the dark of night; well, you would not be too far wrong. However, the energy I felt to be quite exciting and borderline tense. With a candle and holy water at the ready we began. Brid just seemed to know intuitively what to do.

She started by opening up a gateway to allow souls to cross over and the prayers and intention became positively powerful around us. The energy felt like it was being one hundred per cent focused at the task at hand. It was definitely coming from a place of love. I have often heard Bríd say that at the time of crossing of souls into heaven, she can feel their pains or how they died. Images can sometimes flash through her mind of their lifetime on earth.

I have asked her why spirits may not cross over and she explained that maybe they have made a promise to wait for someone or that they believe there is unfinished business they have to attend to. So occasionally souls do need assistance and encouragement to cross over, so they can continue their journey into the next life.

We stood around the monument and we prayed. A few minutes later Bríd asked if I could see the movement of spirits around us from the lights of cars that was passing us by. Can you imagine what they were thinking, driving by us? To be honest it was the least of our problems. I couldn't see anything but I had prayed they would cross. She felt them cross but she was feeling some of their symptoms now.

We strolled back to the car and continued on our drive. We finished it off by paying a visit to St Bridget's Well. No better place to cleanse your hands than a blessed well. Bríd explained the pain she was feeling and it was focused mainly on her stomach. She described the empty hunger pain (from the famine) and also the sickening feeling of TB. As soon as we cleansed our hands, in the dark of the evening her symptoms seemed to settle. It felt great to be a part of something so unusual to most. I'm intrigued by the spirit world so now it's such a normal topic for us to talk about.

That night after a few cups of tea, we hit the hay. I closed my bedroom door and I said a few words of gratitude to God and fell fast asleep. It felt like I had only been asleep a few seconds when suddenly somewhere between deep sleep and being awake I knew I was definitely in another dimension. I knew what I was seeing was a scene from somebody's past but I simultaneously knew I was in the present moment. I spotted (even though my eyes were closed) at the end of my bed a couple standing there very confident and close to each other. She was tall and lean and he was round and plump. I studied them standing there calmly at the end of my bed. All the while I knew my mind's eye was allowing me to see and observe this.

I felt strongly in that moment that I was speaking to them by just simple thoughts. I took a deep breath and I felt calm in their presence. The lady now in front of me was quite tall with a very sleek bob and fringe. Her hair was jet black. She wore a well fitted long jacket and a skirt to below her knees in black. Her face was snow-white, her expression vacant. I knew she was waiting for something. It seemed she had been for some time. I then saw her husband beside her. He seemed sad and incomplete, as if almost anxious about something. His suit was dark wool. He however looked well fed and almost resembled a lord in appearance from back in the day in Ireland. I then question in my mind why they were standing at the end of my bed. Without even a second for my mind to wonder an answer from the tall lady entered my thought space and she transferred the name, Thomas. I was confused and sent my thought back to her and she again passed her thought: it is Thomas the time has come! I must have looked inquisitive when she then nodded towards the direction of my bedroom door.

Immediately I felt Thomas was a young boy maybe about ten years old in spirit. In my mind's eye I glanced towards the door and suddenly a woosh of energy/wind combined with a liquid motion that had a most amazing light appeared at my door. I stared quickly back to the couple who made no reaction as if they could not see this energy ball coming towards me. I felt a little panicked and curious. The energy entered my room and lifted the blankets from my body and swooshed underneath until the energy had the blankets lifted up from me for what felt like a minute or so. The energy was running up my face into my nostrils at such a speed I found it hard for a second to breathe or maybe it was from the fact it felt so cold. I finally just controlled my breathing and relaxed. The energy continued up my face for the longest time and after about twenty seconds or so the energy changed and now had a tropical liquid feel to it.

It no longer had the cold chill it had a second earlier. The energy around my body and face felt amazing! The peacefulness and love I felt from it was simply fulfilling. I really didn't want to wake up. It felt as if you were lying on a tropical beach at the edge of the water and the warm wind was cooling your face with droplets of water in it. I did not want to leave this moment. This was awesome!

My next memory was very gently waking up. I knew immediately it was not a dream. I lay in my bed for a few minutes trying to take it all in. I knew I had to get up and tell Bríd. She would not think me crazy? You know what they say;

if you are not a little crazy, you are mad. As I entered her kitchen I was greeted by the image of Bríd sitting at the table with a tea light candle and prayers being said out loud. I was stopped in my tracks. I asked if everything was all right. She asked if I could hear footsteps in the corridor during the night. I hadn't heard the footsteps and secretly thought "thank God". She said she had to get up to do a crossing because a spirit had come back from the monument in the car with us and for whatever reason he was now ready to be crossed. She said a young boy about ten years old was there and she felt his name was Thomas.

At that very moment I felt my stomach flip and that I needed some grounding because I thought my mind was going to explode. "Seriously does this kind of thing really happen?" was my first thought. "How could she know that?" I finally, after a few stunned seconds, explained my experience which I just had and about Thomas who I believed was just in my room probably around the time she started the crossing and how his parents were at the end of my bed. As we were starting to piece it all together Bríd explained that the energy felt cold on my face as he had not crossed over at that moment and when she had done the crossing for him the energy turns warm. I could not believe my ears. Oh, and that his parents had come to meet him and bring him home.

Bríd has such a beautiful gift that sometimes I think it's not appreciated as much as it should be. I felt privileged to witness what I did but I know in my heart and soul that it was only possible because of being around Bríd and her gift. I realised how important it is to keep souls progressed so they can move onto the next part of their journey. There is no way anyone can even try or suggest to me that there isn't an afterlife or there isn't crossing from one dimension to another because it is simply not true; I have witnessed it. Bríd, you are so appreciated – thank you for all the good you do.

"If it's for you it won't pass you" is one of our local sayings. Last Summer I met a charming American couple who were holidaying in the west of Ireland. This "chance" meeting taught me that, even when I am not doing my work as a healer, if spirit world want my help they will make sure to get it.

BRIDGE OVER TROUBLED WATERS

Elenna Rubin Goodman

10ᵗʰ September 2014

We entered Lisdoonvarna after a solitary drive through Connemara, a landscape simultaneously so spacious and yet completely filled with ancient and historical memory. Like many before us we had stopped at a simple Celtic cross on the side of the road in Doolough Valley. Innocent of information before we were close enough to read the marker, we soon found ourselves in the presence of the Famine as she lives on in the earth of this valley and on the winds carrying those stories still needing to be witnessed and heard. Leaving a few simple offerings and prayers behind, we left with the seeds of a visceral understanding of what this part of Ireland still carries in the flesh and bones of her mountains, water and stones. Fuller understanding of this would come later after meeting Bríd, which would come only after we settled uneasily into Lisdoonvarna and the heaviness began to move in me.

It began as a subtle shortness of breath and a faint tightness around my heart. Rather quickly a grey listlessness filled more and more of my body. For the first time since the start of this journey into and through Ireland a month earlier, I felt a strong need to be somewhere else. Instead, we went in search of food. In the restaurant I immediately felt another swift internal shift. Now I could hardly stay awake. The effort to eat and stay present was beyond what my body could manage. I felt compelled to go somewhere warm and quiet and surrender to sleep. And so we did. The next morning we returned to nearby Ennistymon which had welcomed us so sweetly when we passed through on market morning the day before.

"Maybe it is the loneliness of the land you're feeling," the proprietor of a local café said after I told her about the heaviness that had settled in me. "Tourists come through in the big buses. They pile out, take photos then get back into the bus and leave again. This land has lived through so many leavings. Maybe you are feeling its grief." Picking up the unresolved feelings left behind in a place or among people was not unknown to me and certainly possible here. More than anything I appreciated the invitation to talk so openly about what was happening. And knowing we wanted to explore the area, Claire also gave us directions to the local Visitors Centre, assuring we would be well guided to what we were looking for and perhaps a few more things about which we didn't yet know to inquire.

It was getting on to the edge of late afternoon when we arrived at the Centre and entered easily into conversation with the guide behind the counter. Her name was Bríd. Surely she would be able to direct us to places of interest, and to a few wells in out of the way but nearby places. As Bríd walked us into the auditorium to set up a short film about the history of the land she turned to me and spoke the words that became our shared threshold crossing: "I don't know why I am telling you this. In the six years I have worked here I've never said it to any tourists before, but I am a healer." I smiled and accepted her words as she moved on to start the film.

Minutes later she greeted us in the hall asking if we had any other questions before she went on break. In response I found myself saying, "And I don't know why I am telling you this but ever since I entered this area last night I've been unable to stay fully awake. There's a heaviness on me that shifts in weight and presence but won't leave." Bríd's outer appearance didn't change but something quickened between us.

"A spirit may have settled on you when you arrived," she said simply. I immediately knew that this was so and that it was why she had felt moved, for the first time in six years, to share with a stranger in this public place that she was a healer. She asked if I wanted her help moving it on. I nodded yes and once on break she took us to a private place and began the process of identifying who was travelling with me and what was needed to unbind us.

Bríd entered a deep stillness and from there seemed to feel her way into the identity of the other among us. She said it was a young man and that he wasn't from the famine time though the mark of that suffering was strong in this part of Ireland. She said it felt more like this soul was from the early part of the last century, someone who had died violently. He needed to move on and she asked if he was willing for her to help him do so. He must have agreed because she then began what I can best describe as a moving of energy, along with prayers asking for support and perhaps guidance for this soul to go toward the light. When she was done I felt light and calm. My head was clear for the first time since we had entered Lisdoonvarna.

Then it all came rushing back to me. I could see and feel myself as I was the day before, sitting on a bridge railing. Every part of my being had been wide open with delight when I noticed a small plaque tucked into the stonework of the bridge, naming it as the site where a young man, of the Irish Volunteer Brigade, had been killed in a skirmish with the Royal Scots Regiment in the 1920s. Bríd didn't seem surprised.

So I shared a little more of my story with her. How while travelling through a war-devastated area of Liberia a few years earlier I'd stopped to walk along the bridge over the St. Paul River and was suddenly keening and sobbing. How as suddenly I was completely silent and still. And how our Liberian colleagues who encircled me once the wailing stopped, explained that the water beneath the bridge had run red with the blood from bodies thrown or fallen from the bridge during their civil war, bodies that even still had not yet been properly buried or mourned. Because of her experience working between the realms, Bríd met my Liberian story with ease and immediately understood that I was a hospitable vessel for the ones who hadn't yet crossed and were trying to find their way on.

Over the next few days she generously shared suggestions on ways to care for myself as these uncrossed souls sought me out. The kindness, skill and commitment she showed to supporting souls on their journey beyond their human form was equally offered to one such as myself — one recognised by these travellers as a stop on the way to orienting themselves in their confusion and possible pain.

Over the years I have learnt to expect and accept the unexpected. Yet there are still occasions when even I am totally shocked by what the universe presents me with. The following encounter with a sincere and gentle woman was a strong reminder to me to always take the time to ground and protect myself before doing any healing work.

**

FROM GIZA, VIA ACHILL TO ENNISTYMON

HELENA BOLAND

When I visited the middle pyramid on the Giza Plateau, Egypt in June 2002, I was well and enjoying life. That afternoon I began to feel the first symptoms of what turned out to be a twelve-year illness. I lost all use of my body and became so dysfunctional I spent two years in bed only getting up and coming downstairs in the evenings to lie on a couch. I couldn't have people in the house as their energy would knock me over. I was diagnosed with ME in November 2002. I thought my life was finished.

By 2006 I was well enough to do a little each day and I decided to spend time on Achill Island that summer. I ended up spending nine weeks there altogether and I felt such an affinity with the place, that I could barely drag myself away at the end of August. I was introduced to writing poetry at the Achill Summer School. Now I felt I had some means of expressing the weird things that continued to happen to me since visiting the Egyptian pyramid. The collapse into an abyss of images, sounds and scrambled sensory experiences left me feeling like I was a crazy woman.

In August 2013 as I was enjoying the wedding reception of a relative, my husband was engaged in conversation with a striking woman with white hair, who sat across from me. The woman had her ears open to my conversation with the man sitting next to me, which by this point was about writing short stories and poetry. She directed her question across the table "Do you ever write about spiritual things?" Taken aback I said "no" and continued my conversation, but she again asked, this time more insistently, "But do you ever write about spiritual things?"

I knew she was determined to engage with me, so as soon as I could, I moved beside her, feeling this lady really had something to tell me. She asked me to see a woman in County Clare who could help me: I had been ill with ME for eleven years now and although I had made progress, I was still very cautious about how much energy I expended – having to pace myself in case I became fatigued. At this point I want to say, that since my collapse in 2002 I have had many messengers who stopped me in the most odd places (Oxford Street, London, a casino in Las Vegas) to tell me what I needed to hear, so I had learnt by then to pay attention.

A week later, the lonely raw quality of the landscape in West Clare soothed me, as we drove out from Ennistymon to Bríd's house. My husband drove me, as he had so often, on my many, many travels to find answers. Bríd was younger, warmer and more welcoming than I imagined. I sat on her couch and she asked why there was a dog here. She described the little cream-coloured sheepdog with a nervous disposition. She was describing our family sheepdog from when I was a young teenager. Now she was puzzled and said she usually did not work with animals. After I lay on the table it became clear it was not the dog that needed anything: this little dog had been with me all these years to protect me.

By now I was happy to lie on the treatment table. I felt instantly safe and secure in Bríd's presence. She simply said her prayers with a few candles lit. It all felt so light and then it was as if my left side was being stretched and opened, stretched and opened so much that it was hard to bear. Bríd opened her window and continued praying.

In no time at all it was finished and she invited me to have tea and scones. I can truly say it felt like I had been run over by a bus; I was completely washed out. I knew something had left me and my left side had been expanded from one side of the room to the other.

Bríd said she had crossed over two souls; one was an Egyptian entity and the second a man who may have come from Achill Island. Both of these accounts of spirits who needed to be crossed over made absolute sense to me. I realised I had lived with energy that was not my own since 2002 and even felt the presence of something other than myself, while alone on many occasions. Sometimes I was drawn to dark thoughts of self-harm, but by some saving grace I was able to resist.

In the summer of 2014 I again visited Bríd and this time I was very clear about what needed to be done. A baby who was strangled at birth, and who I believe bore the name Edward had visited me back in 2004. Although I could not see the baby I was aware of the strangling sensation around the throat. I promised to help him then, but had no idea how. Bríd gently crossed his soul over and comforted the father and the mother too so that all three souls could find peace.

Those two encounters with Bríd has left me with the utmost respect and love for Bríd and all she does. She is a natural woman gifted with insight, focus and the strength to work in her very unique way.

One and a half years later I am working with energy myself, offering healing and integration work to others. I want to ask anyone reading this to remain open to the possibility that we humans occupy a myriad of different levels of reality. Bríd travels these with ease and grace for the benefit of all who are lucky enough to be guided to her, as I was.

THE NEXT CHAPTER

My life has taken many turns but I believe I have finally got to where I am supposed to be at this time. I am living the life I am supposed to be living. My various bumps and scrapes, my unhappy school years, being carried unconscious from a smoke-filled building, the night of the attempted assault and robbery, the broken relationships, time spent in Israel, my time reconnecting with nature, the constant love and encouragement from my guides, angels and those in spirit, these have given me the life experiences and the strength to become the healer I am today.

SPIRITUAL HEALING

Teresa R.

Some three years ago I had my first experience of spiritual healing. My best friend had told me about Bríd and arranged an appointment for me, as at the time I was in turmoil emotionally as a result of various family crises.

From the moment I met Bríd, I was struck by the aura of calm and peacefulness that surrounded her. I spent about an hour with her — even though it seemed like five minutes — I could happily have stayed all day! The peace and hope I felt on leaving her home that evening was amazing. Through spiritual healing my awareness of just how powerful the angels can be, has increased a hundred fold. Since then not a day has passed but I have prayed with them and now regard them as my constant guides.

I have had healing sessions with Bríd on a number of occasions since – each experience better than the last. If I cannot make it to visit her I can ring and ask for distance healing. This I find helps to ease my mind and is always hugely comforting.

For me spiritual healing has brought me and mine through many a dark day and night!

I encourage my clients to find the good in their life and to gratefully give thanks for it. I finish each client session, as I do each day, with gratitude.

Now that I am being true to myself I find myself looking forward to the next chapter of my life. I feel privileged that so many people have shared their life stories with me during their healing sessions and for the part I have played in their journey towards healing and progression.

And so, as we continue working on our attitudes to life, how we interact with others, as we learn to see the beauty in ourselves and the world we live in, with a little self-belief we can all progress and find personal healing.

"As it was in the beginning,
Is now
And ever shall be,
World without end"